THE
LAZY WAY *to a*
WONDERFUL
LIFE *– at home*
and at work

GUNNEL RYNER

THE LAZY WAY to a
WONDERFUL LIFE
– at home and at work

ISBN 978-91-985252-0-5

©2019 LYFTA publishing and Gunnel Ryner. All rights reserved.
Translated by Jane Davis, Communicate Language Solutions.
Graphic design: Abel & Co
Illustrations: Eva Abelson
Photographer: Satu Knape, www.fotografsatu.se

1st English edition
Original title: Den lata vägen till ett fantastiskt liv - och arbetsliv.
First published in Sweden in 2017 by Lyfta Förlag.

gunnelryner.com

*A man is alive when he is wholehearted,
true to himself, true to his own inner forces, and
able to act freely according to the nature of the
situations he is in. (....)*

*There is a myth, sometimes widespread, that a
person need do only inner work, in order to be
alive like this; that a man is entirely responsible
for his own problems; and that to cure himself,
he need only change himself. This teaching has
some value, since it is so easy for a man to
imagine that his problems are caused by 'others'.
But it is a one-sided and mistaken view which also
maintains the arrogance of the belief that the
individual is self-sufficient, and not dependent in
any essential ways on his surroundings.*

*The fact is, a person is so far formed by his
surroundings, that his state of harmony depends
entirely on his harmony with his surroundings.*

CHRISTOPHER ALEXANDER, ARCHITECT
– FROM THE BOOK "THE TIMELESS WAY OF BUILDING"

CONTENTS

FOREWORD 11

A FEW WORDS FROM DAVE BUCK 17

CHAPTER 1 INTRODUCTION 21

A tiny seed 21

Thinking positively isn't enough 22

The benefits of being lazy 24

How this book is structured 26

PART 1: ON THE IMPACT OF YOUR ENVIRONMENT 29

CHAPTER 2 THE RIGHT ENVIRONMENT IS MORE
IMPORTANT THAN WILLPOWER 31

Cage or amusement park?

– On rats and treating addiction 32

Helping pensioners to leave their walking aids behind 34

Working environment, buildings, people, society

– all have an impact on us 35

A friendly push 37

How you learn to use a knife and fork 38

Your sister's husband's colleague can make you fat 39

How the lid of a jar can change your behaviour 40

On autopilot 41

Why 80% of all New Year's resolutions are broken 43

Summary 45

Let your environment do the hard work for you 46

CHAPTER 3 THREE BASIC THEORIES ABOUT HOW YOUR
ENVIRONMENT AFFECTS YOU 49

Theory 1: Your environment can hinder you or help
you move forwards 49

Theory 2: You adapt to your environments and your
environments reflect who you are 52

Theory 3: The environment always wins 56

Summary 58

PART 2 : OPTIMISE YOUR PERSONAL ENVIRONMENTS 61

CHAPTER 4 WHAT'S IMPORTANT TO YOU?   63
    Formulate guiding principles   66

CHAPTER 5 YOUR TEN ENVIRONMENTS   69
    Environment no. 1: Physical environment   71
    Environment no. 2: Relationships   74
    Environment no. 3: Networks   78
    Environment no. 4: Financial environment   80
    Environment no. 5: Nature   82
    Environment no. 6: Technology   84
    Environment no. 7: Memetic environment   86
    Environment no. 8: Body   91
    Environment no. 9: Soul   93
    Environment no. 10: Personality   94
    Summary   97

**CHAPTER 6 SEVEN STEPS FOR DESIGNING
OPTIMAL ENVIRONMENTS**   99
    Step 1: Let your guiding principles be reflected
    in your environment   101
    Step 2: Trash your tolerations   107
    Step 3: Cultivate your resources   117
    Step 4: Add what's missing   125
    Step 5: Experiment with your existing environments   132
    Step 6: Try out entirely new environments   137
    Step 7: Adapt to your environments   140
    To do straight away   142
    OVERVIEW – my notes   145

PART 3 : OPTIMISE YOUR WORKING ENVIRONMENT 151

CHAPTER 7 YOUR WORKING ENVIRONMENT   153
    Are you inspired or drained at work?   154
    Physical, organisational and social working environment 157
    Not just health or sickness   157
    Leave that to the Health & Safety people   159
    Take your working environment to a whole new level   161

Creating a good physical working environment 161
Beauty and nature 161
Different environments are best for different tasks 162
Minimise disruptive noise and distractions 163
Environments that promote teamwork,
interaction and recreation 164
Simple ways to increase satisfaction 165
Creating a good organisational and social
working environment 166
Results and relationships 168
Spread a positive infection 171
See, include and care about each other 174
Help each other to succeed 176
Explore and learn from your successes 178
Adopt an appreciative approach 179
Make the most of your strengths 180
Summary 182
What does this mean for you and your colleagues? 183

CHAPTER 8 SEVEN STEPS FOR DESIGNING AN OPTIMAL
WORKING ENVIRONMENT 187
Foundations: Goals, visions and guiding principles 188
Step 1: Let your guiding principles/values be
reflected in your environment 189
Step 2: Trash your tolerations 189
Step 3: Cultivate your resources 190
Step 4: Add what's missing 191
Step 5: Experiment with your existing environments 191
Step 6: Try out entirely new environments 192
Create action plans 193
Following up and carrying on 194
Step 7: Adapt to your environments 194
Discussion prompts to copy 196

CONCLUSION 204

TO THE READER 206

REFERENCES 208
Books and articles 208
Websites 211

" Stop relying so much on you. Design environments that support you and evolve you. "

THOMAS J LEONARD

FOREWORD 11

If you're anything like me, you were brought up to believe that laziness is a negative trait. You probably feel that lazy people are selfish. That they don't want to contribute or play their part. That they simply want to loaf about and take things easy. No, you don't want to be lazy, that's what you've been taught. You feel you ought to fight and struggle and work hard, or you'll never achieve anything.

However, a while back, I began to look at the whole laziness issue in a different way. I've always been a high achiever. I've fought and struggled and bent over backwards and always been at the top of my game, and I've received lots of confirmation of my success. But ten years ago all this came to a screeching halt when I suffered a bad case of burnout. I was on sick leave for five months, which gave me plenty of time to think about my life and myself.

I remember that on one occasion my doctor asked me who I could rely on. "You always cope with everything yourself and support everyone else", he said. "But who supports you?" "Nobody", was my rather melancholy answer. But it wasn't because I had nobody who cared about me – it was because I never asked for help. I was strong, wasn't I? And I could cope perfectly well on my own.

I also remember something my psychologist said, which I first thought was ridiculous, but which has since come to mean a lot to me. She told me to practice being lazy. One day I told her I was going to dig up and move some bushes in the garden, and she said, "Well, I want you to practice digging like a lazy person would. Take a couple of spadefuls, then stop and rest for a while, lean on your spade and look around you. Then take a couple more spadefuls, and lean on the spade for a while again". It wasn't easy for me, but

I practised. I leaned on my spade and I looked around, and it was actually really nice to do things a bit more slowly.

Over the years that have passed since I recovered, I have often thought about the whole 'practising to be lazy' thing, and I've completely changed my attitude to the word. Today, I think laziness can also be positive. In our stressed society, we could probably all benefit from periodically being lazier, giving ourselves time for recovery and doing nothing. Being lazy can also mean being smarter, doing things in the simplest possible way and without wasting energy.

I've also pondered on this whole idea of always having to fight, perform, be strong and clever, and having to cope without help from other people. And I no longer think this is the best strategy. We're constantly fed messages that we should think positively. We're told to set motivating goals, believe in ourselves, that we can do anything we want if we simply have enough willpower and motivation. And yet things don't always go as we want. Perhaps we don't reach those goals. Perhaps we never get that fantastic life we want. My burnout led me to start thinking that there must be a simpler, smarter way of getting where I wanted and having the life I envisaged.

And there is. A couple of years after my sick leave, I took a one-year coaching course at CoachVille, an American coaching institution. And there I found what I'd been looking for. One of the courses I took was called *Environmental Design*, and it gave me an entirely new outlook on how to get where you want in life. The course examined how much we're affected by our environment, and how we can use our environment to help us succeed with change instead of simply relying on our own willpower and self-discipline.

The method was originally developed by Thomas J Leonard, known by many people as the father of life coaching. Leonard was incredibly productive and contributed lots of innovative, almost revolutionary methods and thoughts to what, in the 1990s, was the relatively new area of coaching. He wrote several books and started two coaching institutions; Coach University and CoachVille. He was also involved in founding the International Coach Federation (ICF), the world's largest organisation for professional coaches. When Leonard died in 2003, his colleague Dave Buck took over CoachVille, which he continues to run today.

A few years after I had studied at CoachVille, I had the great good fortune to become a teacher there myself, and was able to further expand my knowledge of environmental design by teaching the method to other people. It was fantastic to see the profound changes and success that the course participants achieved during the 12 weeks of the course. Several of them felt that the course had been 'life transforming', and one said that the course had completely revolutionised both her life and her business.

By this time, Dave Buck had further refined the method and renamed it the *World Power Method*. The expression *World Power* refers to the fact that we can make much greater progress if we allow the world around us to help us reach our goals, compared with relying completely on ourselves and our own *Willpower*.

The concept of environmental design isn't actually a new one. As far back as the 1950s, psychologists were taking an interest in how people's behaviour, health and well-being were affected by their social and physical environments. This was the start of a new independent area of research within psychology, called environmental psychology. And the human-environment interplay is of relevance in other areas too. For example, architects and designers have long known that the buildings they design, construct and decorate have a strong influence on the people who live and work in them. For many years, social psychologists have studied how humans are affected by their social environments – in other words by the people, groups, society and social norms that we surround ourselves with. Researchers also examine the working environment, focusing on how we are affected by the physical, organisational and social environments in our workplaces.

The reason Thomas Leonard's ideas had such a big impact on me is that he transformed this knowledge into a method enabling you as an individual to use your environment to help you more easily get where you want. He also expanded the concept of 'environment' to represent everything around you, but also some aspects of you as an individual.

Unfortunately, Thomas Leonard never wrote a book on environmental design (although some of his thoughts are described, for example, in his book *The Portable Coach*[1]). And even though several other American experts in coaching and personal development have been inspired by and teach Thomas Leonard's theories on environmental design, none of them has written a book about the methodology either. So I decided I'd do it myself. Because these ideas are so good they deserve to be more widely known. You're reading the result.

In this book, I combine exciting research results from areas such as environmental psychology and social psychology, with tips and tools that will help you design your own truly beneficial environment. I have also taken Thomas Leonard's method as a starting point. However, I don't stick to it slavishly. Instead I've included the parts that I've most benefited from myself. I've also adapted and developed the content and added many of my own examples and stories taken from research, my own life experience and from people I have met and organisations I have worked with.

Last but not least, I have added a few chapters on environmental design in the workplace. Because many of us spend a

---

1 Leonard (1998)

large proportion of our time at work, the working environment is perhaps one of our most important environments, with significant influence over both how we feel and how we perform and develop. The book's final section describes how you and your colleagues can work together to create a really good working environment – one that promotes job satisfaction, creativity and motivation, and helps you to reach your shared goals.

I hope that you get as much benefit from the ideas on environmental design as I have myself, and that they make it easy and fun to get where you want, both in life as a whole and at work. That they quite simply allow you to be a little lazier and still get great results.

Happy reading – and best of luck!
Gunnel Ryner
Mjölby: July 2017

"Your environment always wins!"

DAVE BUCK

A FEW WORDS FROM DAVE BUCK

Hi! Coach Dave Buck here with you.

The ideas in the book that you are holding have changed my life many times over. I know that might sound like an exaggeration, but it is absolutely true. In fact, a few of my stories are included in the book.

My amazing friend and colleague, Gunnel, is going to teach you how to design a winning environment for your big game in life and your business or career.

Here is the quick version of the back story.

I first learned about this idea in a program that my dearly departed coach and friend, Thomas Leonard, was teaching, called Personal Evolution. It was based on a concept that he called "the 9 Environments of You". In the program he taught us that we all evolve by adapting to our environments, which are made up of people, places, things and ideas.

The big idea was this: instead of struggling hard to try and change yourself – as we had been taught in numerous personal development programs – it is more effective AND easier to design a supportive and inspiring environment and then simply allow it to evolve you in wonderful and surprising ways. For a culture of people who had been raised on the idea that to achieve anything in life required a LOT of hard work, this was a revolutionary idea!

He told us to look around at our environments and we would see a "picture" of who we would become over time. And that if we didn't like what we saw, we needed to upgrade the environment fast!

I looked around at my environment and was shocked at what I saw! At the time I was living in a small apartment and my roommate was a man I affectionately referred to as "The Cave Man" due to the way he stomped and grunted around the apartment! I thought: if I stay here too long I'm going to devolve instead of evolve.

A few days later, the local newspaper in my area had a big section called "The Lakes of New Jersey" (which were near where I lived in the USA). My girlfriend and I jumped in my jeep and started exploring. By the end of the day I had a new apartment looking out over the lake, and WOW did my life take off in amazing ways from that change.

Since that time I have been constantly guided by the idea that the best way (and also the lazy way) to achieve something is by focusing on designing the environment first. This life-changing concept guides both my business and personal life in powerful ways.

As I mentioned before, the ideas that you are about to explore were first created by my coach and friend Thomas Leonard. Thomas is often referred to as the "Founding Father" of professional life coaching. For 5 years I spoke with Thomas on the phone every day. We traveled together and led many coaching events together. One powerful way you can accelerate your growth is to hang around someone on a mission to change the world! As you will learn in a few pages, Thomas was a life-changing relationship environment for me!

In another example of a powerful environment, I was assistant soccer coach for a major university team for 14 years. The head coach of the team was Manny Schellscheidt, who is in the US Soccer Hall of Fame. Manny is credited with creating the first US soccer coach licensing school. Manny always said that the primary job of a coach is to create an environment where the game comes to life. That is so profound! So you can see that the way I became a great coach was by putting myself in environments with great coaches. You can find a way to do the same thing for anything in life that you want to "become".

When I want to create something new in my life, the first thing I do is upgrade my environments. Another example is that, 5 years ago, when I wanted to expand my life and create new business possibilities, I got an apartment in New York City. Being in this energy has propelled me into some powerful opportunities. I love it so much.

So, coming back to this book, you are in very good hands with Gunnel! Gunnel is one of the best teachers we have ever had in our school. We loved having her, and you are lucky to have her now as your guide.

DAVE BUCK

MASTER CERTIFIED COACH, MBA, CEO OF COACHVILLE
NEW YORK: AUGUST 2017

*"Environment
is stronger
than willpower."*

PARAMAHANSA YOGANANDA

CHAPTER 1

INTRODUCTION

A tiny seed

Imagine you're a tiny seed. Inside you is all the potential you
need to grow into a tall, flourishing tree. But to do that, you have
to be planted in a favourable environment, with fertile soil, water,
nourishment and sunlight, protected from pests and hard winters.

If, instead, you have the misfortune to be sown in a barren, dry and windy environment, you may have to accept only growing into a dehydrated little bush. It makes no difference how positively you think, how much you struggle and how much you want to be that tall, flourishing tree – your environment limits what you can achieve.

But if you were magically transplanted to that favourable environment, do you think you'd need to think positively and struggle with your own motivation to turn into a tall, fine tree? Almost certainly not, because your environment would help you to grow and develop. You wouldn't have to make any effort at all.

Of course you're not a seed, you're a human being. But you're also affected by your environment; the physical places you find yourself in and the things, people, ideas and circumstances that you surround yourself with. Everything and everyone in your life either supports you to get where you want and become the person you want to be – or not.

The advantage in being a person rather than a seed is that you can change your environment and design it so that it's as favourable as possible. Of course you can't affect everything in your environment. And the extent to which we feel we can make an impact also varies between individuals. We face different circumstances in life, and we have different opportunities. But regardless of what your life's like, you can often do quite a lot to change your environment, and even small changes can have big effects. And unlike that tiny seed, you can even choose to move yourself and completely change your environment.

Thinking positively isn't enough

These days, there are plenty of resources for anyone who wants to work on their personal and professional development. There are thousands of self-help books, inspirational talks and courses in mental training, positive thinking, self-esteem, believing in yourself, how to reach your goals... and lots more besides. A great deal of this is practical and useful, but it puts almost all of the focus on you. And if you want to develop and reach new goals and you're only focusing on what's inside you – your own willpower, motivation, self-esteem, self-confidence, perseverance and drive – then you're only doing half of the job. And the half that requires the most energy, too.

With this book I want to give you the part that's often overlooked when we talk about personal development – you can call it the other half, or the missing link. The fact is that your environment is perhaps the most powerful, and also the most neglected, catalyst for change in your life. And this is true both in life in general and at work.

As humans, we develop by adapting ourselves to the world around us, and your environment is therefore crucial in determining whether or not you'll succeed. An environment that's full of obstacles, or which can't give you the vital support you need, makes it difficult to create long-term change. But if you review and redesign your environment so that it supports you in what you want to achieve and gives you inspiration, energy and a boost in the right direction, you don't have to rely on your own willpower and can instead simply glide along. Thomas Leonard, who first developed the method, used to say, "You can delegate your success to your environment". In other words, if you create as good an environment as possible for yourself, it will help you move forwards. It's a bit like going down a slide towards your goals instead of constantly having to struggle uphill.

Do you want to create sustainable change? Do you want as good a life as possible – both at home and at work? And do you want to do this in an intelligent and simple way that makes you less dependent on your own willpower and self-discipline? Then I think you'll find this book useful.

The benefits of being lazy

Laziness is often seen as a negative character trait, something to be ashamed of. Lazy people avoid making an effort, don't want to help and think only of themselves. They're passive and want everything served up to them by other people.

But as I wrote in the foreword, I've started to look differently at the whole concept of laziness. I think laziness can also be useful. That in fact there's a healthy, intelligent way to be lazy that we could all benefit from trying out now and then.

With all the stress around us, my feeling is that we could all do with taking a little more time for rest and recovery. The expression 'idleness' – doing absolutely nothing but being indolent and unoccupied – has recently become popular again. This isn't a new idea, but a classic philosophical notion that is once again being highlighted as a way of creating space, relaxation and time for reflection in our so very fully booked days.

Being just lazy enough can also mean using your time intelligently. In other words, doing things as simply as possible and using the least possible amount of energy. Conserving your energy and your resources and finding simple, creative ways of getting things done. Bill Gates is supposed to have said: "I choose a lazy person to do a hard job. Because a lazy person will find an easy way to do it".

With this book, I want to show that there's an alternative to the classic view of personal development and how we can create a good life. I'm amazed that this classic view focuses so much on struggling and straining, using willpower, being disciplined and persevering, when so much research shows this isn't always sufficient – and that in any case there's a much easier path. A path that often seems to have been forgotten.

So when I use the expression 'lazy', it doesn't mean that we should quit our jobs, close down every workplace, hospital and road construction project and simply go home and lie in the hammock, stop helping other people and live an entirely passive life. Instead, I mean that we should make it easy, fun and inspiring to get where we want, and that the path there involves using our environment to help us by consciously reviewing and designing it to give us a helping hand in the right direction.

This doesn't mean that we should never make an effort or get sweaty and tired. But we don't need to see this as negative. Instead, it should be easy and feel enjoyable. And perhaps we won't even be conscious of the effort, because we don't need to use willpower or self-discipline. We simply go along with the flow. Rather like when I'm out dancing. Dancing is a fantastic form of exercise, and you get really quite sweaty and breathless doing it. But I never think of it as exercise or a tedious effort, because I have such a great time when I'm dancing.

Of course, reviewing and designing your environments means that you need to do some work. It won't happen by itself – you need to take responsibility for making sure it's done. So to begin with you'll have to put in some effort. But once you've made the changes you want, the reward will follow, and you can just sit back and enjoy your environment as it helps you move forwards.

"Progress isn't made by early risers. It's made by lazy men trying to find easier ways to do something."

ROBERT HEINLEIN

How this book is structured

The aim of this book is to give you both inspiration and concrete tools and tips for designing truly optimal environments that help you move in the direction you want. You can read it as a factual or inspirational book, but it also contains exercise sections so you can use it as a workbook.

PART 1 of the book gives an overview of some of the research and knowledge about how we are affected by our environments; an impact that's much greater than most of us probably imagine. This section also describes three basic theories of how the environment affects us, formulated by Thomas Leonard and Dave Buck.

PART 2 takes an individual perspective. It discusses your personal environments, how they affect you and how you can review and revise them so that they support you in getting where you want. It also contains some exercise sections where you can go through your own environments and note down your thoughts and ideas about how you want to redesign them. If you choose to work through these exercise sections, by the time you finish reading the book you will have drawn up a complete, personalised action plan.

PART 3 takes a more collective perspective and describes how you and your work colleagues can review and develop your joint working environment. The working environment is an environment that you often share with other people. This means you can't just consider yourself and how you want your environment to be. Instead, you and your colleagues must combine and adapt your various needs and wishes. Here, too, there are exercise sections that you can do together with your colleagues, or with your employees if you're the manager. Even if you're primarily interested in the section on the working environment, I recommend that you first read Parts 1 and 2, as they will give you an important foundation and many useful insights that will help you redesign your working environment.

PART 1:

ON THE IMPACT OF YOUR ENVIRONMENT

" Success, not to mention personal evolution, becomes sustainable when there are environments and failsafe structures that support it.

After all, who wants to rely on fortitude and willpower to get things done or to develop oneself?"

THOMAS J LEONARD

CHAPTER 2

THE RIGHT ENVIRONMENT IS MORE IMPORTANT THAN WILLPOWER

When I first encountered Thomas Leonard's method for environmental design, it was a real eye-opener for me. I have a degree in behavioural science and should really have been conscious of how much we're affected by our surroundings. But over many years I'd been indoctrinated by books and courses on personal development, which all insisted that it was down to me to be motivated and persistent and to have lots of willpower. Now it suddenly became clear that there was another, simpler and more intelligent way. The method I learned at CoachVille also made me curious to learn more. Was there any research that supported Leonard's theories?

Quite a lot, it turned out. Our environment's influence on us has been the subject of many studies within a large number of research fields. I think it's important for there to be a scientific basis for anything I teach, so even though the focus in this book will be methodology, I still want to take the research as our starting point. In this chapter I highlight a number of exciting and thought-provoking examples from various areas of research to give you an image of the enormous extent to which our environment has an impact on us, and how it affects our life and behaviour in ways that we perhaps aren't always conscious of. In the next chapter, we will take a closer look at Thomas Leonard's theories and the actual methodology for environmental design.

Cage or amusement park?
– On rats and treating addiction

Let's start by looking at how a really poor environment can create hopelessness and even lead to drug abuse, while a really good environment helps us to flourish.

In the 1960s, researchers did a number of experiments involving rats, to study the mechanisms behind drug-dependency. The most common method was to place the rats in small, cramped cages, completely isolated from each other, and to give each rat two bottles of water – one with pure water and one laced with morphine. The result was that the vast majority of the rats preferred the morphine mixture, and pretty much all of these rats eventually killed themselves with overdoses. Researchers claimed that this showed how incredibly addictive morphine, heroin and similar drugs are.[2]

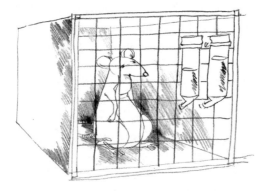

But in the late 1970s, this conclusion was questioned by a Canadian researcher and psychologist named Bruce Alexander. He said that just like humans, rats are social animals, and that isolating them in small cages without companionship or the opportunity for activity could almost be equated with torture. If so, it wouldn't be so surprising that they would choose to numb

---

2 Alexander (2010)

their consciousness with morphine. Alexander and his colleagues decided to create a completely different environment for their lab rats – a paradise for rats in the form of a large enclosure 200 times bigger than the normal cages. It had straw on the floor, nature designs on the walls, lots of tunnels, balls, exercise wheels and other toys, ample quantities of cheese and other food and, above all, a load of other rats that they could play with, socialise with and have sex with. The rats absolutely loved their new environment, which the researchers called 'Rat Park'.[3]

Here, too, the rats were offered two bottles. One with pure water and one with water laced with morphine. And what do you think happened this time? Yes, in Rat Park, almost all of the rats chose the pure water. None of them became addicted, and none of them took overdoses.

Alexander's conclusion was that the rats' environment, with its opportunities for social contacts and activities, was what made the difference. Drug-dependency, he said, was perhaps not primarily caused by the power of the drugs, but by the environment. If your life feels like you're a prisoner in a small cage, perhaps you're more inclined to use drugs than if you experience your life as one huge amusement park.

3 Alexander (2010)

In Portugal, similar conclusions have been reached. In 2000, Portugal had major drug problems. One per cent of the population were drug addicts, which was one of the highest levels in Europe. So they decided to revolutionise addiction treatment. Instead of taking the traditional approach and focusing on the individuals, punishing them to try to motivate them to stop taking drugs, they chose to focus on their environment. Addicts are now offered care instead of punishment, and help to create as normal a life as possible, with work, housing and social interaction. And this has produced fantastic results. By 2015, the use of injected drugs had fallen by 50% and the number of overdoses had dropped dramatically, as had the number of HIV cases.[4]

Now this book isn't going to be about addiction, but I think that these examples show very clearly how much we are affected by our various environments and how important it is to get support from those environments when we want to create change, instead of the responsibility always being placed on the individual and their own willpower and motivation.

Helping pensioners to leave their walking aids behind

A nursing home in Oslo provides another example of how a change of environment can stimulate change in the people in that environment. At Manglerudhjemmet, they have radically changed the environment for the residents. With simple means and almost no budget, they transformed a large, very impersonal institution into something more like a true home. First they replaced the furniture. They also created a cosy restaurant, a spa, a shop and a football-themed pub. The staff even worked with the residents to brew beer. They took inspiration from the Hogewey dementia village in the Netherlands: an enclosed mini-society with a café, restaurant, food shop, hairdresser's salon, pub and theatre. The concept of dementia villages has now spread to around ten other

---

4 Hari (2015)

countries. At Manglerudhjemmet, the new environment has had a number of positive effects on the residents. For example, centre manager Hilde Helland explains that when the elderly men arrive in the pub, they are suddenly no longer bothered by pain in their hips. They don't need their walking aids, but jump up onto barstools and swing their legs as if they were 20 again.[5]

Working environment, buildings, people, society – all have an impact on us

It's not merely within addiction research and elderly care that we've begun to understand the importance of a sound, supportive environment.

When we think of environments that affect us, we probably most often think of our working environment. Research has been carried out in this area since the early 1900s, and has strongly contributed to our current awareness of the importance of the working environment, and to the laws and regulations that have developed within this area. The research includes everything from studies on how the physical working environment affects us, to studies of stress and other problems linked to the psychosocial working environment. As working life has changed and been transformed from an agricultural and industrial society to become increasingly dominated by the service sector, the focus of working environment research has also moved from areas such as ergonomics, loads and chemical risks to mental illness and stress. Research has contributed to many improvements in our working conditions, but we still face major challenges in coping with escalating instances of sick leave linked to stress and other psychosocial factors in the workplace.

Another major interdisciplinary area of research, which in the 1950s grew into an independent area within psychology, is environmental psychology. This includes research into how people's behaviour, health and well-being are affected by their social and physical environments. Physical environments consist both of the

---

5 Søhoel & Hanssen (2016)

natural world and of environments constructed by humans, such as workplaces, housing, hospitals, schools, playgrounds and all types of public space. Social environments are the people, groups and societies we have around us. These have also long been studied within social psychology and sociology. One of the foundations of social psychology is that human behaviour is largely affected by external factors, and not merely by internal processes. At the same time, according to researchers, we are often unconscious of the extent of this impact.[6] Psychology professor David Myers says that social psychology has provided the field of psychology with a meaningful social context, which helps us to better understand people's thoughts, emotions and behaviours.[7]

Environmental psychology emphasises the mutual nature of the relationship between humans and their environments. While we are affected by our environments, we also have the opportunity to both change and choose them. If we understand how people are affected by their environments, we can also learn how to design them to be as optimal as possible. And conversely, by studying how people modify and choose their environments, we can learn more about how they are affected by them. One example is that we now know a view of natural surroundings is good for human well-being and performance, and that it can be helpful to design buildings so that they offer such views. And by studying where people choose to live, we can understand the

*"We shape our buildings
and afterwards
our buildings shape us."*

WINSTON CHURCHILL

---

6 Clayton & Saunders (2012)
7 Myers (2014)

types of environment in which they are happiest and healthiest.[8]
Environmental psychology is an important area of research,
not least for social planners and politicians. For example,
researchers studying the causes of the obesity epidemic in the
USA have found many explanations in the environment. A
few of these contributory factors include increased access to
fast food; technical developments such as microwave ovens;
increased taxes on tobacco, leading to more people replacing
cigarettes with comfort food; and towns built for commuting
by car, with long distances between homes and workplaces,
leading to a great deal of sitting in traffic jams. One important
task for researchers, social planners and decision makers is to
try to create good environments that encourage residents to be
physically active and to develop more healthy behaviour.[9]

A friendly push

The research area of behavioural economics, which studies
how psychological and social factors affect people's financial
decisions, is today taking a growing interest in 'nudging'. Nudging
is a way of encouraging human behaviour to move in a desired
direction without preventing people from making other choices.

Researchers have realised that we humans rarely make
entirely rational decisions in which we consciously weigh up
the advantages and disadvantages against each other. Instead we
are governed by a number of other, often unconscious factors,
such as habits, norms, how different alternatives are presented,
what people close to us are doing and signals relating to immediate
reward. In other words, factors in our environment. Nudging is all
about giving a friendly push in the right direction by designing
choices so that it's easy to make the right decision. This method
is primarily used within areas such as health, environment and
sustainability, but companies and organisations are also starting
to become aware of nudging.

8 Clayton & Saunders (2012)
9 Stokols (2014)

One example of a successful nudge was a hotel chain reducing the size of its plates, encouraging people to take less food from the buffet – thereby reducing food waste by 20%. Another is a study carried out at Roskilde University in 2011, in which stickers were installed representing green footprints leading to the nearest rubbish bin, reducing the amount of rubbish discarded on the ground by 46%.

Still another popular method for nudging is preselection – in other words, the alternative you ideally want people to choose is already ticked. One example of this is the American company that tried out automatically registering its employees in a pension plan to make them save more for their pension. The plan meant that part of the employees' salary was set aside for their pension every month. If they didn't want to take part, they were perfectly free to leave, but they had to actively choose to do so. The experiment was a success, leading to more people saving for their pension – something that most of us think is important but which we tend to put off for later because retirement age seems so far away.[10]

How you learn to use a knife and fork

When it comes to our social environments, there's a great deal of knowledge about how they affect us. One area which has been the subject of many studies and theories is the socialisation process, the process through which we adapt to people – our parents and then to our playmates, school friends, workmates and other groups – and integrate the norms, values and cultural patterns that they represent.

The socialisation process continues throughout our lives, and it is this process that teaches us how to behave and function in the group, society and culture we live in. Without socialisation, we would have no language; we wouldn't know how to use a knife and fork or other tools, we wouldn't know when to sleep or what to sleep on, what is appropriate to eat for dinner or what constitutes

---

10 The facts about and examples of nudging are taken from Frizell (2017) and Petersson (2014)

suitable clothing in different contexts, to take just a few examples.

But of course these expectations, norms and rules all vary between different societies and cultures. If you change your environment and end up in a completely different culture, you are exposed to resocialisation. This is what happens, for example, if you go to prison or enter another institution, when soldiers go to a country at war, or when they come home from the same war, or if you move to a new country as an immigrant. In these circumstances, you are forced to leave behind parts of your old identity and habitual behaviours and to learn to act on the basis of completely new norms and expectations.[11]

Your sister's husband's colleague can make you fat

Another, related area in which many exciting studies have been carried out is how our social network shapes us. One of the most pioneering books in this area is Nicholas Christakis and James Fowler's *Connected: The Amazing Power of Social Networks and How They Shape Our Lives*.[12]

In their research, Christakis and Fowler have demonstrated that our attitudes, emotions and behaviours in a large number of areas – everything from election participation and cooperative behaviour to smoking, weight increase or reduction and happiness – are clearly affected by other people in our network. And the most startling of all is that it's not merely your own friends that affect you, but also your friends' friends and your friends' friends' friends. Even if you've never met them. So in other words, your sister's husband's colleague can make you fat, despite the fact that you've never met.

Christakis and Fowler call this *The Three Degrees of Influence Rule*. This means that everything we do or say tends to be spread further and 'infect' other people in our networks, three steps from ourselves. If your friend's friend stops smoking, or your friend's friend's friend gains weight, that spreads through the network and

---

11 The facts on socialisation and resocialisation are taken from Little (2013)
12 Christakis & Fowler (2010)

also affects you. And the same thing applies if you make a change in your own life. If you start to go running, or become a more pleasant and more cooperative person, that spreads through the network and can affect hundreds or even thousands of other people.

In their mathematical analysis of social networks, Christakis and Fowler have also looked at how happiness spreads. They've demonstrated that if one of your friends is happy, that increases your own chances of being happy by 15%. And the spread of happiness doesn't stop there. If your friend's friend is happy, that increases your chances of happiness by 10%. And if your friend's friend's friend is happy, that also increases your chances of happiness by 6%. Maybe that doesn't sound like much, but imagine the effect it can have on you if many of your friends' friend's friends are happy.

Based on this, I feel it's important that we all think about what we spread through our networks and infect those around us – and those around them – with. If we spread happiness and kindness, we affect other people positively. And those positive ripples eventually come back and have a positive effect on us.

How the lid of a jar can change your behaviour

One area that's related to nudging, which I described earlier, is research into how an environment's physical design controls your behaviour. For example, if you're eating at a buffet and it's organised in one way, you'll choose to eat certain dishes. If it's organised in another way you'll choose other ones. Google did an experiment in its New York offices. The staff were used to having free access to M&Ms from open baskets in the office. But Google decided to try to get its employees to eat fewer sweets. So the open baskets were replaced with opaque ceramic jars with lids. The lids were really easy to open, but the consumption of M&Ms in the office still fell dramatically – over the following month, 3 million fewer M&Ms were eaten. All thanks to a simple lid.[13]

---

13 Ariely (2010)

Everyone who works with retail marketing knows how to affect our behaviour through environmental design. Shops are fitted out in a carefully calculated way that optimises our desire to buy. Retail marketing researcher Jens Nordfält says that there are many tricks to encourage us to buy more. I'm sure you've experienced the phenomenon of popping to the shop to buy a carton of milk... and coming out with lots of things you never intended to buy. According to Nordfält, two-thirds of all of our purchasing decisions are made as we walk around the shop.[14]

Within the convenience goods sector, it's well known that you can radically increase sales of a product by changing how it's exposed and where it's positioned on the shelf. Nordfält explains that our eyes often come to rest 15 degrees below horizontal, so that if you move a product to a level somewhere between the customer's waist and their chin, you're likely to quadruple sales. And by moving the sweetcorn, washing powder or ketchup from the shelf to the end of the aisle, sales can increase by up to 1000 percent. As well as physical positioning, retail marketing people work with colours, scents – for example freshly baked bread – and music, all to stimulate our desire to buy.[15]

Music is also used in the restaurant industry. A fast-food restaurant that wants to increase customer turnover will play high-tempo music so that we eat and leave more quickly, making space for new customers. More expensive restaurants often have calmer, more pleasant music, which makes guests relax, stay for longer and order more to eat and drink.[16] How do you think bar owners get you to drink more? It's simple – they turn up the volume of the music. The louder the music, the more difficult it is to have a successful conversation, and so you drink more.[17]

On autopilot

The majority of us probably like to think that we make our own decisions, but in fact we spend almost half of our lives on

14 Nordfält (2007)
15 Nordfält (2007)
16 Stokols (2014)
17 Guéguen (2008)

autopilot, and then it's the design of our environment and our habits that control what we do, not conscious decisions. This has been demonstrated by several researchers, including psychology professor David Neal and his colleagues.[18] Autopilot means that we do things automatically without consciously needing to think about what we're doing, and in these circumstances we generally do what's easiest and doesn't require any tough decisions. For example, we pick up a tin of sweetcorn because it appears in our line of sight, or take the first dish that looks good on the buffet.

The fact that you have autopilot turned on for so much of your time has effects not only on your behaviour, but also on your love life. I apologise in advance for crushing your romantic expectations of meeting 'the one', but a study by researchers Michèle Belot and Marco Francesconi demonstrated that who you choose to date is only 2% determined by what you actually want and 98% by who happens to be nearby.[19]

Nobel Prize recipient and psychologist Daniel Kahneman is one of the researchers who have demonstrated that humans aren't as rational as we'd like to believe. Kahneman divides our thinking into System 1 and System 2. System 1 corresponds to autopilot – the quick, unconscious, automatic thinking that doesn't require any effort and is constantly active. It's System 1 that means we can drive a car and talk on a mobile phone at the same time without thinking about what we're doing. System 2 is the slower, more rational, conscious, logical and deliberate thinking that requires more effort and is therefore often switched off. It's only called in when System 1 isn't enough; when we need to handle more complex or unusual situations. So the system we most often rely on, System 1, bases its conclusions on our previous experiences and on emotions. It reuses things we've done before and tries to protect us from being scared or sad.[20]

When you use System 1 and operate on autopilot, you're being controlled by your context; your environment. The environment contains many signals – what are known as triggers – which make

18 Neal, Wood & Quinn (2006)
19 Belot & Francesconi (2006) i Harford (2008)
20 Kahneman (2012)

you do as you always do in that particular environment. And it's these that control your behaviour, not your own intentions or goals. It's also these triggers in the environment that mean you stick to your habits. If you have a vending machine in the break room at work that sells chocolate and from which you normally buy something sweet to go with your coffee, the vending machine has turned into a trigger for you. The mere sight of it triggers your habitual behaviours, and in a few minutes, without even having to think about what you're doing, there you are with a chocolate bar in your hand.

According to David Neal and his colleagues, the key to changing your habits is in your environment, not in more willpower. If you change your environment so that your triggers disappear or become more inaccessible, you reduce your risk of falling back into your old habits.[21] Compare this with the Google experiment – when they made it more difficult to access the sweets, it changed the employees' behaviour. In short, don't try to change yourself, change your environment – it's much simpler and more effective.

In the example with the vending machine at work, that might mean asking your employer to get rid of the vending machine, to move it to another place where you don't have to look at it, or perhaps to fill it with something more nutritious.

Why 80% of all New Year's resolutions are broken

We all know that we're healthier if we eat well and take regular exercise. Doctors in particular should know this. And yet 44% of male doctors in the USA are overweight.[22] I can't count the number of times I've heard friends say that from now on they'll start exercising, reduce the time they spend on social media, sleep for eight hours every night, spend more time with their children, stop procrastinating, stop eating junk food or watch less TV. Often nothing happens at all, or they manage to stick to the changes

21 Neal, Wood & Quinn (2006)
22 Kalb (2008)

they've decided to make for a couple of days before they fall back into their old habits. And I'm no better myself – I decide almost every morning to go to bed no later than 10 o'clock, but almost never succeed in doing so. It makes you wonder how difficult it can be. And it turns out that the answer is: very difficult. 80% of all New Year's resolutions are broken, according to a study of 15,000 people carried out by FranklinCovey.[23]

The reason so many of us find it difficult to stick to the changes we've decided to make is that we try to rely on our willpower. And willpower is a limited resource; many studies show that the more we use our willpower, the weaker it becomes.

Social psychologist Roy Baumeister and his colleagues carried out an experiment in which they instructed their research subjects not to eat anything for a three-hour period before they came to the laboratory. When they arrived at the lab, the participants were divided into three groups. Group 1 was given a plate of chocolate cookies, which they were told not to eat, and a plate of radishes, of which they could eat as many as they liked. Group 2 was also given both cookies and radishes, but they were told that they could eat whatever they wanted. Group 3 was given nothing at all to eat.

After putting up with these circumstances for a while, the participants were given the task of solving a set of geometrical puzzles. They were told the puzzles were simple, but in fact they were puzzles that could not be solved. The results showed that the participants in groups 2 and 3 struggled with the puzzles for much longer than the participants in Group 1, who quickly gave up. According to Baumeister, the reason was that the participants in Group 1 had used up all their willpower on resisting the tempting cookies, and so they quite simply didn't have sufficient willpower left to struggle on with the tough puzzles. Even the participants in Group 3, who were probably quite hungry by this time, managed to carry on for longer.[24]

Our willpower is constantly tested in everyday life, and the more we use it the weaker it gets. So it's not so surprising that

---

23 Parker-Pope (2007)
24 Baumeister et al (1998)

we often choose the path of least resistance, which means that we fall back into old habits and comfortable routines. Instead of going out on that morning jog before work, you stay in bed for an extra half an hour. Instead of doing everything you intended to do after work, you end up as usual on the sofa with a Netflix series on the TV. And instead of making a healthy salad, you take a packet of crisps with you to the sofa.

Psychologist Shawn Achor says that the best way of dealing with our lack of willpower is to make sure that the path of least resistance leads to the desired behaviour. By changing your environment, you can ensure that the things you want to do become simple and easily accessible, while simultaneously making the undesired behaviour more difficult. Do you want to increase your chances of actually going out on your morning jog? Lay out your running clothes and put your running shoes right by the bed, so that they're easily accessible when you wake up. Or even better, sleep in your running clothes so that you only need to put your shoes on when the alarm goes off. Do you want to watch less TV? Take out the batteries from the TV remote control and put them in a drawer in another room. Do you want to eat more healthy food? Then fill up your fridge with nutritious, easily prepared food, always have a bowl of fresh fruit available, and hide the packets of crisps on a high shelf in the garage – or even better, don't have any crisps at home at all.[25]

Summary

What I wanted to show with this chapter is that there's a great deal of research and knowledge about how strong an influence our environment has on us. We've seen how lab rats take to drugs when their environment is depressing, but refuse them when they have stimulating surroundings. We've seen how elderly people blossom and forget their aches and pains when their accommodation becomes more pleasant and more like the life they used to have.

25 Achor (2011)

We've taken a quick look at some of the research areas studying how our environment affects our behaviour – everything from working environment research to environmental psychology, sociology and behavioural economics. We've seen how we are affected by physical places, both natural and artificial, and by society and the groups, people and norms we surround ourselves with. We've seen that we are affected by people in our social network, even if we've never actually met them ourselves.

We've looked more closely at what actually controls our behaviour and seen that we aren't as rational as we perhaps might think, but instead that we are often on autopilot, allowing triggers in our environment to control us – and how this is used both in marketing and by social actors to give us a push in a particular direction. And finally, we've also seen that willpower is a limited resource, which means that we often choose the path of least resistance.

Let your environment do the hard work for you

This is just a small sample of the extensive research and knowledge available on the subject, but I think it's enough to make it clear that we are products of our environment. And doesn't it strike you as odd that, despite all this knowledge, we don't talk more about how we can use our environment to more easily get where we want and create good results?

If we're so strongly affected by our environment, then we also need to understand that the road to success isn't about more willpower, self-discipline or positive thinking – but instead about reviewing and changing our environments. The lazy (and intelligent) way to a wonderful life, both at home and at work, means creating a truly favourable, supportive and inspirational environment and then simply allowing it to do the hard work for you.

"There's just one way
to radically change
your behavior:
radically change
your environment."

BJ FOGG

THREE BASIC THEORIES ABOUT HOW YOUR ENVIRONMENT AFFECTS YOU

In the previous chapter, I gave you an overview of just some of the research into our environment's influence on us. In this chapter, before we look at the actual method in more detail – in other words, what you need to do to create truly optimal environments both for yourself and together with your colleagues at work – I want to describe a few of Thomas Leonard's thoughts about environments, some of which have been expanded upon by his colleague Dave Buck, who has now taken over and runs CoachVille. The methodology I recommend for designing your environments is based on three basic theories formulated by Thomas and Dave. So to start with, let's have a look at each of these three theories.

Theory 1:
Your environment can hinder you or help you move forwards

The first theory states that everything in your environment can either hinder you or help you move forwards. In other words: If you try to move from Point A to Point B, the environment can make it easy or hard for you. If you have a high wall or a mountain between you and your objective, that's an obstacle. If instead you are sitting at the top of a slide and the objective is at the bottom, your environment will take you there effortlessly. In fact, you'd have to actually struggle against your environment not to reach the bottom of the slide.

Of course what we want are environments that support and inspire us and help us move forwards, so that we get more of a feeling of being on a slide through life, and not having to deal with things that hinder us or drain our energy.

An obstacle needn't be a physical one, like a mountain or a wall, but can be anything at all that holds you back. For example, it could be a partner or friends ridiculing you and laughing at your dreams and ambitions, or norms and values in your family or society telling you not to stand out. Have you ever been in a workplace with a really negative atmosphere? Where the most common comments are "it was better before", "you can't do that", "what's the point of this" and "what on earth have they come up with now"? Or perhaps you had a job where you felt that you were regressing rather than moving forwards? No stimulation, no way of using your expertise and strengths, no opportunities for learning. Those are just a few more examples of environments that hold you back.

Fortunately, there are also environments that are exactly the opposite, which give you energy, help you move forwards and make it easier for you to develop. My good friend Dave Buck once told me about when he went on a training camp in Bolivia. It started when he spotted an advert for a summer camp for football players at the Tahuichi Academy in Bolivia. Dave had played football his entire life, and when he saw this advert he thought "Yes, I have to go there, what a fantastic chance to develop as a football player!" So he rang up the contact person. It turned out that this was a camp for young football talents between 15 and 21 years of age – and Dave was 33. But he somehow managed to get a place and travel to Bolivia, where just like all the other youngsters he lived with a host family. His host parents were a year younger than he was, but that didn't bother Dave.

All day, every day, throughout the entire month, was filled with training. Sometimes the players were taken to tall sand dunes which they had to run up and down, while other times they went on runs through the jungle or along riverbeds, did technical exercises or played matches. The training was incredibly tough and demanding, but Dave described how he had a feeling that he didn't need to do very much himself other than be where he was told to be and do the exercises they were told to do. His experience was that he simply 'went along' and did everything the others did – and in any case, it was fun. As he put it himself, "If I'd decided myself to train hard on my own for a month, it would have required enormously more self-discipline and willpower, and I certainly wouldn't have gone to the beach to run up and down sand dunes".

When he came home from the camp, it was soon time for a match with his own football team. Dave went out onto the pitch, and to the amazement of both his teammates and himself, he completely dominated the match. He dribbled past his opponents like a modern day Pele, scored goal after goal and outclassed all the other players on the pitch. His teammates were astonished. "What's happened to you?" they asked. And Dave himself couldn't explain. "I have no idea! I've been in Bolivia, running up and down sand dunes!" It was only then that he realised how much he'd developed as a football player, simply by putting himself in another environment for a month. He'd achieved a completely different level to his former team mates, and soon realised that he needed to move to a better team to maintain that change. So he applied to a team in a higher division – and they accepted him.

Environmental design is about creating your own Tahuichi Academy – an environment that makes it easy for you to grow and develop in the direction you want. And that environment can be very different for different people. Perhaps you don't want to become a fantastic football player, but you undoubtedly want to achieve something. So what would an optimal environment be for you?

Perhaps you have a very clear image of what that optimal environment would look like. But it may also be the case that you don't have any idea. Sometimes you perhaps have to think completely outside the box, dare to be irrational and seek out environments where you've never been before. If someone had advised Dave how he could become a better football player, they probably wouldn't have said, "You need to go to Bolivia and run up and down sand dunes". Sometimes you have to dare to experiment, launch yourself into things and try something completely unexpected, just to see what happens.

Perhaps you think that Dave's story seems a bit off-topic. Wasn't this going to be a book about the benefits of being lazy? Well, remember what I wrote in the introduction: the laziness I encourage you to try in this book isn't about simply lying in your hammock and being passive. Instead it's about no longer having to rely on your own willpower and motivation to get things done. It's about putting yourself in an environment that helps you move forwards and makes it feel fun and simple – even if that also means that you have to put some effort in.

Theory 2:
You adapt to your environments and your environments reflect who you are

This theory states that you are affected by your environments and that, simultaneously, your environments are affected by you. Just as in the metaphor of the tiny seed that I described in the introduction, you adapt to the environments you find yourself in. For example, if you move to a new place, go on a course or start socialising with new people, the environment will affect you. As soon as you enter the new environment, you start to adapt to it.

Imagine that you're starting a new job or a new school. Consciously or unconsciously, you adapt to the new environment. The atmosphere, jargon and routines quickly become established for you. In the best case, it's a positive environment where you can be happy and flourish. In the worst case, it's an environment that drains you and makes you a shadow of your former self. Imagine going on holiday to a tropical paradise island. Or going to a concert by your very favourite artist. Or going to prison. Each of these environments would naturally also affect you, and very quickly too.

We adapt not least to the people we surround ourselves with – something I discussed in the previous chapter. A number of researchers have demonstrated that the groups you belong to determine what type of person you are, and that the very simplest way of achieving change in yourself is to surround yourself with other people who already have the habits, behaviours and character traits you want to adopt. We often have a negative image of group pressure, but group pressure can be something good if you make sure that you're in the right group. For example, it has been shown that low-performing students who share their accommodation with high-performing ones achieve improved grades. And doctors have seen that if all they do is to give their patients lists of advice for how to live more healthily... well, not much happens. But if the patients spend more time with other people who already live more healthily, behavioural change happens automatically.[26]

In other words, you are who you hang around with. So take a close look at the people you spend the most time with. Do you like these people? Do you want to be like them? Because that's

26 See, for example, Achor (2011), Friedman & Martin (2012), Christakis & Fowler (2010)

what you'll be like, if you aren't already. And if the people around you don't reflect who you want to be, perhaps you need to find new friends.

At the same time that you're affected by and adapt to your environment, the process also happens in reverse. Over time, your environment begins to reflect who you are. When you have been in an environment for a sufficiently long time, it will reflect you as a person. If you look at a person's environment, you find out a great deal about them. If I was to meet your closest friends, or come to your house and see how you live, I would probably be able to create a reasonably accurate image of you.

One important aspect of this theory is that the adaptation process is quick, while the reflection process is slow. Let me give you an example to make this clearer.

Have you ever gone on a course, a workshop or another event, where the entire environment was so inspiring that you felt you'd changed as a person? You meet fantastic new people, learn loads of exciting things and perhaps start thinking in completely new ways. The food is good, the conversations are interesting and the surroundings are beautiful. And you quickly adapt to this inspiring environment and think, "Wow, my life has completely changed. From now on I'll live according to all the great things I've learned here!"

And then you come home to your normal environment, and what happens? Yes, after just a few weeks – perhaps even just a few days – you're back in your normal routines and you're exactly the same person you've always been.

Why is it so difficult to maintain inspiration and stick to the changes you've decided to make? Well, because when the course is over you go back to your old environment, and that hasn't changed. It's exactly the same as it was before. As soon as you come back, you adapt back to the old environment and become exactly the same person you were before you went on the course.

But why doesn't your old environment reflect the inspired person you now are? Because the process is slow and months or even years can pass before it's complete. And over that time, you've lost the inspiration you gained from the course.

To maintain your state of inspiration, you need to change your old environment before you re-adapt to it. You need to add things, places or people to your old environment which remind you of what you want to do, help you to retain that energy and motivation and make it easy to continue on your new path. And you need to get rid of things that sabotage you.

For example, imagine that you've been on a fantastic writing course. You're full of ideas and inspiration, and now you really want to write a book. One way to make sure that your environment supports your ambitions is to create a writing corner for yourself at home – a space that's so cosy and inviting that it acts as a magnet and you can barely keep yourself away from it. You can also draw up a clear plan, day by day, that you display in a clearly visible place, where you can tick off your success. You can join an online writer's group or stay in contact with some of your new friends from the writing course so that you can continue to support, encourage and help each other onwards.

'Don't focus your motivation on doing Behavior X. Instead, focus on making Behavior X easier to do.'

BJ FOGG

The point is to change your environment, to remove some of your old triggers and add new ones, so that your environment reminds you of your goals and makes what you want to do easy, and what you don't want to do difficult.

Theory 3:
The environment always wins

The final theory is that your environment always wins over willpower. As we discovered in Chapter 2, in Roy Baumeister's experiment with cookies, radishes and impossible puzzles, willpower is a limited resource.[27] But your environment just keeps going. It has no such limits.

We can only rely on willpower for a limited time. Sooner or later it runs out. Constantly fighting an uphill battle or struggling against a headwind often leads to you eventually running out of steam, giving up and adapting to your existing environment.

So you have to take control of your environment – otherwise it takes control of you. If you want to achieve lasting change in yourself, you also have to change your environment. You must create winning environments; environments that support you in what you want to achieve, inspire you and help you move towards success. In this way, you adapt to what you want.

Now, perhaps you'll object that history is full of stories of people who have actually succeeded in overcoming tough environments and conditions and who have achieved fantastic things. And of course it's possible to overcome a tough environment with the help of incredibly strong willpower – but it's not very effective because it requires so much energy. It's much better – and more intelligent – to try to achieve an environment that's on your side.

In personal development circles it's often said that you can achieve anything you want if you simply set goals and have sufficiently strong self-discipline and motivation. If you do this you can achieve fantastic things like climbing Mount Everest,

---

27 Baumeister et al (1998)

ideally barefoot and wearing a blindfold to make it an even greater challenge. And then cycle the whole way home again afterwards. On a unicycle.

But if I look at my own situation, the problem is that I just don't have that willpower and motivation. I'm quite indolent. These days, I'd even say that I'm essentially lazy. And I may be wrong, but I think that the majority of people are a bit like me. I'll never climb Mount Everest barefoot. I'll never even do it wearing a pair of stout boots. Not even if I had a full support team, with guides, porters, my own masseur and a Michelin chef. I might just manage to climb up the nearest hill to where I live, which is all of about 250 m high. With my shoes on. And the chances that I might do that would increase dramatically if I had people around me who took me along with them and made it feel like a fun day out. For us ordinary mortals, who lack that extreme willpower, it's much more intelligent to take another look at our environment and allow it to give us a boost in the right direction. Why rely only on your own self-discipline – which you already know is a limited resource – and almost kill yourself struggling, when you can instead glide through life, simply by ensuring that you have a good environment?

Of course this doesn't mean that an optimal environment will make everything simple for you. It can also contain challenges, which inspire and encourage you to make a bit more effort – but your environment will still be helping you forwards. As I have said earlier, the lazy way doesn't mean that you simply lie around passively in your hammock, but that it should be fun and easy to do what you want. But this assumes that the challenges are the right sort and the right size, so that they stimulate you rather than making you give up.

Sometimes life and the conditions facing you are so tough that it can be difficult to believe you really can affect your environment. But you can almost always make some small modification in your environment that can make life a little easier, and then build on it with another little change. One small step at a time. And once life is a little easier, you can try making bigger changes to create a really good environment, which can act as a buffer against the tougher periods in life.

Summary

Now we've looked at the three basic theories relating to how our environment affects us:

Theory 1: Your environment can either hinder you or help you move forwards. A poor environment is full of obstacles and things that drain your energy. A really good environment inspires you, supports you and makes it feel like you're simply gliding along, without having to expend so much of your willpower and self-discipline.

Theory 2: You adapt to your environments and your environments reflect who you are. The first of these processes, that you adapt to your environments, is a quick one. As soon as you put yourself in a new environment, you will be affected by it. The second process, that your environments reflect who you are, is slower. It can take months or even years, but your environments gradually begin to reflect who you are, so that even someone who doesn't know you can get a picture of you simply by looking at your home or at the people you surround yourself with. For a change in yourself to be sustainable, for example if you've been away on an inspiring course, you also need to immediately change your old environment, so that it supports your new, inspired you.

Theory 3: The environment always wins. Willpower is a limited resource, and sooner or later it runs out. But your environment lasts for ever. It has no limits. So you have to take control of your environment and make sure that it's on your side. Otherwise it takes control of you.

– Does your environment help you move in the
   right direction?
   Or do you have to constantly struggle uphill?

– Do you have any examples of times when you put
   yourself in a new environment and quickly changed
   to adapt to it?

– If you look at your environments as they are today,
   how have they affected you?
   Who have you become by adapting to your current
   environments?
   How does that agree with who you WANT to be?

– If you could design an environment that would
   help you move forwards, what would it include?

PART 2:

OPTIMISE YOUR PERSONAL ENVIRONMENTS

*"There is only one success
— to be able to spend your
life in your own way."*

CHRISTOPHER MORLEY

CHAPTER 4

WHAT'S IMPORTANT TO YOU?

This part of the book describes how you can create really great, favourable environments for yourself, in your own life. You'll learn more about your own personal environments and how they can be designed to support and inspire you and make it easy for you to achieve the life you dream of.

To get as much as possible from this section, I want you first to stop and look at your own life for a moment.

The majority of us have some kind of goal we want to achieve. It can be a very concrete goal, such as getting a job as a sales person, running 10 km in 50 minutes, achieving a turnover of €100,000 in your own company, giving up sugar or writing a book.

It might also be a slightly more vague dream or vision of how you want your life to be and who you want to be as a person. It can involve things you want to achieve or the way you want to develop as a person, but it can also mean just wanting to feel good and be satisfied with life.

For one person, perhaps it's important to build a successful career, earn lots of money or achieve a high status in society. For someone else, it may be the opposite, and they feel it's important to work less and have a good balance in life. It can also involve you wanting to live in a way that's in line with your most important values. It can mean being able to be healthy and satisfied with your life. Or being a good parent, partner or friend. Or something completely different.

Ralph Waldo Emerson, American author, poet and philosopher, wrote the following:

"– To laugh often and much;

*– to win the respect of intelligent people
and the affection of children;*

*– to earn the appreciation of honest critics
and endure the betrayal of false friends;*

– to appreciate beauty;

– to find the best in others;

*– to leave the world a bit better whether
by a healthy child, a garden patch,
or a redeemed social condition;*

*– to know even one life has breathed
easier because you have lived.*

– THIS is to have succeeded."

I think that's very nicely put. But there's no one life goal or definition of success that's more right than any other. So as you read this book, try to think about what's important to you. You don't even need to call it a goal. It can be a wish, a vision, a dream or an important value.

Regardless of what this is to you and what you choose to call it, I want you now to think about your own dreams and ambitions in life, in the short or long term – or both. This will help you to get the most out of reading this book.

Set aside plenty of time and write down your thoughts on the following pages. If you come up with more goals, dreams or visions as you read the rest of this book, simply come back and add them here.

....

....

....

What goals do you want to reach over the slightly
longer term (5-10 years)?

....

....

....

....

Think about what's important to you.
When you look back on your life on your 90th birthday,
how do you want to have lived?

....

....

....

....

....

....

Who do you want to be?
What kind of person do you want to develop into?

....

....

....

....

....

....

....

Formulate guiding principles

If you were to try to summarise your image of who you want to be and how you want your life to look in a number of short phrases, what words would you use?

Put together a few short phrases that capture the essence and energy of your goals for how you want to live and who you want to be as a person. You should ideally formulate them so that they contain a lot of energy and emotion and so that they remind you of where you're heading. Try to write two or three phrases, each with three to five words.

I call these short phrases your guiding principles. We will come back to these and use them again further on in the book.

Below, I give you a few examples of what guiding principles might be. View these simply as inspiration – it's important that you find your own phrases to summarise what's important to you in particular.

EXAMPLES of guiding principles:

Inspirational, creative energy source

Curiosity and learning

Happy and full of life

Enthusiastic, bright entrepreneur

Presence and enjoyment

Give and receive love

Write your own guiding principles below. If you want to change, add or remove some of them as you read this book, simply come back to this page.

My guiding principles:

....

....

....

....

....

....

....

....

"Be always with people who inspire you; surround yourself with people who lift you up."

PARAMAHANSA YOGANANDA

YOUR TEN ENVIRONMENTS

As I mentioned earlier, this book isn't about just one environment, but several. In fact, almost everything around you can be regarded as an environment. I've chosen to divide them up into ten different environments.[28] In this chapter you'll learn more about these ten environments, what they consist of and what it's important to think about when you review and develop your own environments. After the description of each one, there are questions to help you reflect on your own environments. In the next chapter you'll learn a concrete seven-step method to make all of your environments as optimal as possible.

Your ten environments are:

External environments:

Physical environment

Relationships

Networks

Financial environment

Nature

Technology

Memetic environment

Internal environments:

Body

Soul

Personality

---

28 Thomas Leonard originally defined seven environments, which were then expanded into nine. In recent years, Dave Buck has merged two of the original environments – 'Nature' and 'Soul' – and added a new one – 'Technology'. I have chosen to keep 'Nature' and 'Soul' as separate environments and have added 'Technology' as the tenth environment.

Each of these environments can contain things that give you energy and help you move forwards. They can also contain obstacles and irritations that drain your energy and hold you back. Perhaps some positive things are missing that you can add to achieve a really optimal environment.

All of your ten environments are represented both in your leisure time and at work or school. In this section we will focus on how you are affected by and can change your own environments both at home and to some extent even at work. In the book's third and final section, we will examine in more detail how you can work with your colleagues to make your shared working environment as favourable as possible.

Of course, the division into ten environments could have been done in many different ways. The important thing is to understand that pretty much anything can be seen as an environment, and to create as broad and comprehensive an image as possible of everything that can form part of your environments.

The first seven environments are external ones, while the last three environments – body, soul and personality – can be called your internal environments. The internal ones largely correspond to what you can read about in many other books about personal development and health. These are therefore not the primary focus of this book, but I have chosen to include them anyway to give you a comprehensive picture and because it can give you new insights if you think about them as environments you find yourself in.

But what's the real point of seeing everything as an environment? It makes sense to see my surroundings as an environment, but my own personality, body and soul? Isn't that going a bit too far? Well, that's an understandable point of view, but the idea is that by regarding these as environments you can more easily achieve some distance from them and see how they affect you – and that you actually can change them, at least to a certain extent.

Let's now go through each of the ten environments and see what they can include.

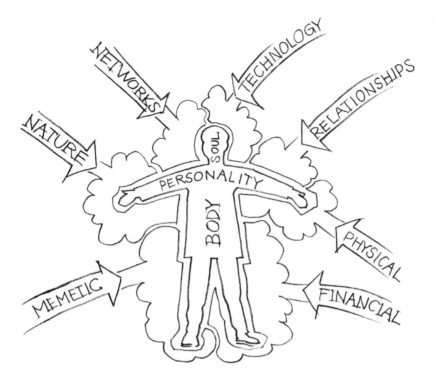

Environment no. 1: Physical environment

Your physical environment consists of things and places such
as your home, your physical workplace, your car, furniture,
pictures, ornaments, tools, toys and other possessions –
everything you can touch.

Designing a good physical environment involves creating
security, beauty and harmony around us. We also want our
physical environment to be functional, to help us be effective
and to make life as easy as possible for us. It should contain
machines, aids and tools that work and there should be enough
space for our things, together with some form of structure,

so that we know where our possessions are. The physical environment should support you by making things you want to do simple, and things you don't want to do difficult.

Your physical environment affects you much more than you may realise. It should ideally help you to feel good on all levels, give you warmth, relaxation, security and make you feel alive and full of energy. Your physical environment may also express your personality, so that you get the feeling, "Oh, this is really me. I feel at home here!"

Of course the physical environments that satisfy different individuals and make them feel good aren't all the same. Some people like living in small flats close to other people in the inner city, while others feel better in a house with no neighbours in the countryside. What suits one person is a source of stress for another. According to sociologist William Michelson, it's important to start from what suits each individual. He uses the expression *congruence* to describe how well a person's physical and social environments agree with that person's goals, needs, cultural norms and activities.[29] What type of physical environment suits you best?

Environmental psychologist Daniel Stokols claims that your physical environment reveals a great deal about your personality and that we often judge people on the basis of their environment. At the same time, your personality and behaviour are shaped by your environment, which means that the environments you have grown up in become part of your identity. This applies to your home, the towns you have lived in, the schools you have attended and the sports halls or other places where you have spent a lot of time. Stokols also states that different environments affect different people in different ways depending on their personalities and the types of environment they are accustomed to and happy in. An environment with lots of people, noise and impressions can be stressful for one person yet stimulating for another.[30]

Your physical environment affects you not only on the conscious level, but also unconsciously, because all the places and things you

29 Michelson (1970)
30 Stokols (2014)

surround yourself with send out different forms of metaphorical

73

messages to your subconscious. Take the example of the heap of papers you have sitting on your desk. Perhaps it signals to you that you aren't on top of things and that you run the risk of forgetting something important. A shelf full of books you haven't read can mean different things to different people. It could signal a feeling of a lack of time and that you can't take the time to read the books although you really want to. Or perhaps it's a feeling that the shelf contains lots of opportunities and experiences that you're looking forward to exploring. A wall full of diplomas, certificates, prizes and awards might foster a feeling of self-confidence and pride, and remind you that you have fantastic resources and talents and can achieve anything you want. Or perhaps it's the opposite, and you get a guilty conscience because the diplomas are old and you've stopped striving for new successes.

REFLECTION: *What does your physical environment look like?*

– Look around you in your home and examine the things you surround yourself with. What do you feel when you're in the different rooms in your home, looking at the room and your things? Do you like what you see?

– Is your physical environment designed in a manner that helps you maintain focus, or does it create chaos and confusion? Do you feel inspired and full of life? Or do you instead feel drained, irritated or frustrated?

– What messages do the various parts of your physical environment send to you?

– What's your physical environment like at work? How about in the car? And in other places where you often find yourself – perhaps you have a caravan or mobile home? Or perhaps you spend a lot of time in the gym, the local community centre or somewhere else? How do you feel in these environments?

Environment no. 2: Relationships

Your relationship environment consists of the five to fifteen people who are closest to you – the people you meet every day or almost every day. We can call this your inner circle. It includes your family, your closest friends and the colleagues you work with most. If you have a coach or mentor, they can also be part of your relationship environment.

These people have a strong impact on your ability to achieve your goals and become who you want to be. So it can be a good idea to reflect on the following questions:

Do they inspire you?

Do they know about your dreams and goals?

Do they support you?

Do they challenge you in a good way?

A friend of mine was going to start his own business and happily told me how his partner supported him 100% in planning to become self-employed. But when his income was significantly lower for several months in a row, his partner changed her mind and said, "You need to get yourself a proper job again and forget about these ridiculous plans". This doesn't count as 100% support.

*"Keep away from people who
try to belittle your ambitions.
Small people always do that,
but the really great make you feel
that you, too, can become great."*

MARK TWAIN

When you review your relationship environment, you shouldn't
just consider which people inspire you or give you support and
push you onwards – you should also think about how the people
you spend time with affect your own personality.

Two years ago, my daughter moved to Norway to work there
for a few years. This was something she had dreamed of doing
since she left school a couple of years previously, but it hadn't
become reality. One of the reasons that it hadn't happened earlier
was that she had no friends who wanted to go with her. But then
she met a new friend, who turned out to dream of doing the same
thing. Suddenly my daughter was full of new energy and the two
girls began to plan to travel to Norway together. It was fantastic
to hear my daughter when she spoke about her new friend with
great enthusiasm. "It's so cool, she brings out sides of me I'd
almost forgotten I have. She makes me into that positive, energetic,
enterprising and fearless person I really want to be, and who I've
lost over the last few years!"

Do you also have this kind of person around you – someone
who brings out the best in you? Hang on to them – they're worth
their weight in gold! As you read earlier in this book, the people
you are closest to have an enormous influence over how you
yourself think and act. We adapt to and become like the people
we socialise with. For example, research shows that over time

you develop the same dietary and fitness habits and even the same career ambitions as the people you have around you. If you're in a group of people who have really high goals, your own bar will be raised too. And this also applies in reverse. If your friends aren't particularly ambitious, your own ambitions will also be lower.[31]

I've seen many examples of how our own social circle can affect us. One woman I coached described how she had gradually been drawn into the culture of complaint that permeated the group she exercised with, where a major aspect of the community was complaining about everything they could think of. My client really didn't want to be like that, as she was essentially a very positive person, but she had been affected on a subconscious level. When she became aware of how much she had adapted to that environment, she decided to try out a new form of exercise so that she could meet other, hopefully more positive, people.

Another coaching client felt incredibly frustrated about his work situation. All his colleagues felt the same, the situation was chaotic and there was no hope of improvement as the problems were caused by external circumstances outside the company's control. The frustration in the group had finally turned into resignation and passivity. My client described it as a swamp he was slowly being sucked into. He had long tried to fight against it, to change things and to keep his spirits up, but a lot of time had now passed and no improvement was in sight, so he was beginning to run out of energy. "Who do you want to be?" I asked him on one occasion. "Happy, enthusiastic, optimistic and full of energy", he replied. "And what kind of people do you spend most of your time with?" I continued. "The tired people among my colleagues", he said. "And then I go home and fall asleep on the sofa because I've just had enough."

We agreed that he needed to find a strategy to avoid wasting more energy than necessary on what he couldn't affect at work, to save his strength so that at least a couple of days a week he could meet the kind of person he himself wanted to be.

---

31 Flora (2013)

Someone who could stimulate the best in him, somebody to
be inspired by, to toss ideas around with and who could bring
out the person he had the potential to be. He also decided to
look for a new job. A year later he moved to another, much less
chaotic department in the same company, where there was a
more positive atmosphere among the staff, and today he's much
happier and more like the person he said he wanted to be.

REFLECTION: *What does your own relationship environment
look like?*

- What type of people do you want to adapt yourself to?
  Who do you want to be?

- What kind of people do you spend the most time with now?
  How do they affect you? Do you like these people? Do you
  want to be like them?

- What people do you have in your surroundings who bring
  out the best in you?

- Do you have any role models who inspire you?

- Do you have people with similar goals to you, so that you
  can encourage each other?

- Do you have people close to you who believe in you,
  who know about your goals and support you in every
  way they can?

- How can you spend more time with the people who
  affect you positively?

Environment no. 3: Networks

Your network environment consists of all the other people you are
acquainted with, outside your inner circle. They can be other
friends, acquaintances, work colleagues, business contacts,
network contacts or people in the same groups as you.
For example, there are groups with:

> Shared values, such as a church or charitable
> organisation.
>
> Shared opinions, such as a business network.
>
> Shared interests, either leisure or professional.
>
> Shared experience, such as alumni associations
> from university.
>
> Shared geography – the people who live in
> the same area or are part of the same residents'
> association, for example.

Everybody you know by name and greet when you meet them
counts as a member of your network environment. The majority
of us have a significantly larger network than we may think. I
once read somewhere that every adult Swede knows on average
800 people – and that was before social media arrived on the scene.
Perhaps the figure is even higher now.

The network environment is an environment full of
opportunities. The people in your network can support you,
answer questions, introduce you to other people, recommend
you for or tell you about jobs or assignments. The more
influential people you have in your network, the better. When
I say 'influential', I mean people who are respected, who may
have a large contact network themselves, and who can give
you opportunities – for example by introducing you to other
people – but who can also take opportunities away from you.

As I said in Chapter 2, we are strongly influenced by the people we have in our network, not only the ones we have a direct connection to, but also by their contacts and their contacts' contacts. Emotions, opinions and behaviour spread and infect other people in the network as far as three steps away. This means that some of the impact you're exposed to is outside your control. You can't do much about what your work colleague's sister's best friend thinks or does, which can then spread throughout your network.

What you can do something about is the people in your network that you choose to spend the most time with. You can also choose to seek out new contacts who you think will make you happy and benefit you and add them to your network.

REFLECTION: *What does your own network environment look like?*

– When you look at your network environment, does it contain people who act as role models, who inspire you and help you move forwards?

– Do they know what you want to achieve? Have you asked for their support? Do they share their experience and top tips? Do they challenge you in a positive way?

– How can these people from your network help you to achieve your goals and become who you want to be?

– If you became like the most influential people in your network, who would you be?

– What other groups would you like to be part of? Which other people would you like to have in your network? What's holding you back and preventing you from making contact?

Environment no. 4: Financial environment

Your financial environment includes everything to do with money, such as your income and outgoings, any savings and investments you may have, your routines for managing your finances, various types of security system, such as insurance policies, unemployment cover, health care cover, pension funds, and whether you have a buffer that means you can cope with unforeseen expenses. It also includes people who help you manage your finances, such as bank contacts, financial advisers and insurance advisers, and various tools or services such as accounts software, internet banking and your own budget if you have one. An important part of your financial environment is also your own approach to money and your thoughts and convictions relating to money and finance.

Your financial environment affects you in many ways, not least your feeling of freedom and security. For example, constantly worrying about whether you have enough money takes up a great deal of energy. If you know that you have enough to cope, even if something unforeseen happens, you can spend your energy on other things.

For some people, earning as much money as possible and increasing their financial prosperity is a strong driving force. For others, just having enough to make ends meet is sufficient. For my part, money has never been a very strong driving force – as long as I know that I have enough for my everyday needs, I'm happy. But if I don't, money suddenly becomes something that takes up a large share of my thoughts and a great deal of my energy. As a self-employed person I have seen both feast and famine. During some periods I've had enough money to spend it almost as I want without having to think about it much. But I've been through times when I've worried night and day about how to make ends meet and not known if I'd be able to pay my bills on time.

For some people, perhaps a tough financial situation can lead to them pushing themselves even harder. For me it's the opposite – I think about the situation a lot but get nothing done.

I'm unable to act because of the stress. To me, a secure financial environment is a precondition for being able to devote my energy to developing myself and achieving my goals. At the same time, I'm not concerned by the fact that life as a consultant, speaker and author means I can't do much in terms of advance planning and that I never know what my financial situation will be in six months' time. I can cope with this, largely thanks to a kind of basic trust and my experience that things usually come out right in the end. I suspect that for many other people, the uncertainty I live with would be terrible and that they couldn't imagine living without a fixed, secure and stable income. We simply have different approaches to our own financial environments.

Many people live on the border of poverty and find it difficult to make ends meet. Of course this is stressful and takes up a great deal of energy, and it also affects their opportunities to make changes in many of their other environments. Regardless of your financial situation, it can be sensible to take an overall view, perhaps to draw up a budget, so that you have a grasp of your income and outgoings and know what your limits are, which helps avoid a good deal of worry. And remember that many changes in your other environments needn't cost anything.

REFLECTION: *What does your financial environment look like?*

- What's your financial situation? And what are your thoughts about your finances? Do you have a sufficient buffer to feel secure even if something unforeseen were to happen? .

- Do you have good tools, procedures, insurance policies and advisers?

- How do you need to manage your finances so that they help rather than prevent you from reaching your goals?

Environment no. 5: Nature

This environment includes everything that forms part of nature, such as flowers, plants, trees, parks, lakes, the sea and watercourses, animals, pets, the seasons of the year, the weather, the sky and the stars.

Nature exerts a strong attraction on humans. We are fascinated by beautiful rainbows, gleaming stars in the night sky, panoramic views of beautiful landscapes or the sound of waves crashing on a sandy beach. Most of us have favourite places in nature – places and environments where we relax, top up with new energy and gain new inspiration. Having contact with and being in nature makes us feel more alive, gives us calmness, harmony and joy, and helps us recover.

Nature also has positive effects on your health. Being in a forest environment lowers your levels of the stress hormone cortisol, reduces your pulse rate and blood pressure, improves your immune defence and also decreases feelings of anxiety, depression and fatigue. In Japan, 'forest bathing' has been part of the national public health plan since 1982. The idea of forest bathing is quite simply to be present among trees, without doing anything particular. You don't need a step tracker or to do any type of exercise – the point is simply to be, to sit still and rest or stroll slowly. Forest air doesn't merely feel fresher and better – the fact is that the trees and other plants exude various essential oils that protect them from bacteria and insects. And inhaling these substances has been shown to strengthen the human immune system.[32]

Regularly spending time in nature has a range of other positive effects too. You become more creative, you improve your memory, you perform better – you even become slightly more intelligent.[33]

If you can't get out into nature, simply having a view over nature through a window can help. A study of patients in a hospital compared those who had a view of a group of trees from their room with patients who had a view of a brown brick wall. The

32 Livni (2016)
33 Keller (2005), Wiseman (2010)

patients with a view of nature recovered more quickly, took lower doses of pain relief medication and had fewer complications. They also had fewer negative comments from nurses in their medical records (such as "upset and crying", or "needs a lot of encouragement") and instead had more positive ones (such as "in a good mood" or "up and moving about well").[34]

Several years ago, I read an article in our local newspaper in which the columnist wrote about the demands we place on our home. He had had a man from Kenya as a guest for a little while, and this man had first stayed with a friend who lived in a flat in a tower block in the centre of town. He didn't like it there and had found it difficult to settle in. When he was able to stay with the columnist in a simple holiday cottage without modern comforts, he was much happier. When the columnist asked him what was important for him in a home, he said, "I don't have any big demands. The only thing I want is to be able to walk straight out through the door and sit down by a tree".

That statement struck a chord in me. Immediately I read it, I thought, "That's how I feel too". Despite my having been born and grown up in a completely different environment than this Kenyan man, the two of us have something that unites us, something that has been with the human race since the beginning of time – an attraction to nature.

Even if you aren't out in the forest or by the sea every day, you can have contact with nature, for example by going to a park; sitting under a lone tree in the centre of town; taking a little while to look out at the clouds through your window; playing with your dog or cat or other pet; growing flowers, herbs or vegetables on your balcony; pottering in your garden, or as simple a thing as buying a bouquet of flowers to put on your kitchen table. Simply placing a potted plant on your desk or hanging pictures of the natural world on the walls has positive effects on your health and well-being and makes you more creative. Or even buying a green pen. Writing with green ink has actually

34 Ulrich (1984)

been shown to increase your creativity.[35] Although I'm doubtful whether green ink has any direct positive effects on your health.

REFLECTION: *What does your own natural environment look like?*

- How much time do you spend in nature? Enough to recharge your batteries?

- What's your favourite place? Is it a special place or type of place, for example forest, meadow, sea or garden? How does it make you feel?

- How can you get more of nature and its positive effects into your indoor environments? At home and at work?

Environment no. 6: Technology

This environment consists of your technical aids and virtual places. Technical aids include everything from computers of all sizes and shapes, mobile phones, tablets and GPS right down to digital fitness trackers, games consoles and VR glasses. Virtual places include all types of social media such as Facebook, Instagram, Twitter, LinkedIn and YouTube, game worlds such as World of Warcraft and other online games and internet-based groups, forums and platforms where you interact with other people. We can probably agree that this is an environment that has had an enormous influence on us in recent years.

Your technological environment opens up endless opportunities for learning, communication, social interaction, information-collection and entertainment, and gives you the opportunity to be constantly connected and have access to everything you want simply with a few touches of a screen. Today's technology has given us enormous freedom and flexibility. We can work where

---

35 Wiseman (2010)

we want, keep track of what's going on with our family, relatives, friends and the rest of the world, and we can control a lot of the technology in our homes from our mobile phones. We can also get across our message and advertise our products and services in a completely different way. It's almost impossible to understand how only 20 years ago we could cope without mobile phones a nd computers.

Of course, all of these technical aids and our constant connection also bring with them risks and negative consequences. We are constantly reachable, we have constant access to our work email and are perhaps even expected to use it in our free time. At the same time many of us complain about stress and a shortage of time. According to the 2016 study *Swedes and the Internet*, the average Swede spends an hour a day on Facebook and other social media.[36] And if we look at the younger generation, they spend even more time on social media and on keeping in touch with their friends via various apps on their mobiles. Many young people keep their phones in their hand – or at least close to them – more or less all the time. At the dining table, on the toilet, in the bath and even while they sleep. Many people, both youngsters and adults, compare themselves with other people's successful façades on social media and feel that they are failures. We're also so busy updating Instagram or Facebook when we're doing something fun that we sometimes forget to actually enjoy it in the moment.

The technological environment has developed enormously in just a few years, and this is probably only the beginning. I mentioned VR – virtual reality – above, where by wearing a pair of special glasses, we can enter a completely different environment. But now there's also AR, which stands for augmented reality, and involves adding virtual components to our actual world. Pokémon Go is an example, in which you walk around a town and your telephone shows you the same environment that you have before you, but with small Pokémon figures on park benches, fences or walls. Both of these technologies are being developed at incredible

36 www.soi2016.se

speed, and who knows – in a few years time perhaps it will be hard for us to distinguish between the real world and virtual ones.

The concept of digitalisation can now be found everywhere, and increasing numbers of services and tools are becoming digital. The technology is being developed constantly and experts say that we face major changes that will permeate our entire society and affect all of us. Digitalisation leads to fantastic opportunities but also brings with it concerns, for example relating to how jobs and the labour market will be affected and how all the data collected about us can be used. Some people are warning about the gulf that can arise between those who are on the technology train and those who are being left behind. Constantly updating your digital skills will be crucial, both for organisations and for us as individuals.

REFLECTION: *What does your technology environment look like?*

- What benefits do you gain from your technical aids and virtual places such as social media? How can they help you achieve your goals?

- How does constant connection affect your ability to be present in the moment, to focus and get things done, and to wind down and relax? How do you find a balance?

- What do you do to keep up with developments and to update your digital skills?

Environment no. 7: Memetic environment

The expression *meme* was originally coined by British evolutionary biologist Richard Dawkins in his book *The Selfish Gene*.[37] A meme is an idea, a behaviour or a style that spreads from one person to another in a culture. Memes are often described as the cultural or mental equivalent of genes. While genes are spread

---

37 Dawkins (1976)

and replicated biologically from generation to generation, memes
are also transmitted from generation to generation and in our
culture, but they are spread in other ways. We see and take in
ideas from our surroundings, we imitate and follow traditions,
habits, practices and routines. These can be convictions,
assumptions, norms, behaviours, religious beliefs and other ideas
around us. We're also exposed to an enormous amount of ideas
that are spread through a range of sources of information and
knowledge, such as books, advertising, the internet, newspapers,
the TV, radio, blogs, podcasts, films and music. Memes are also
found in organisations – where we often call them 'company
culture'. They frequently involve us doing things in a particular
way, without knowing why and without questioning them
because "this is how we've always done it". They can also
involve explicit rules, norms and values in the organisation.

You have perhaps heard the expression 'internet memes',
which is usually defined as a concept that is spread widely via
the internet and which becomes popular and well-known. But
in fact, everything that's spread via the internet is a meme, if
you use Dawkins' own definition. The internet is also a very
influential source of ideas, which of course has both advantages
and disadvantages. There is currently a great deal of discussion
of 'filter bubbles' – in other words, sites such as Facebook and
Google serving us the kind of thing they think we will like and
which confirms the opinions and the world view we already
have, with the result that we live as though we are in a bubble
and miss a lot of what goes on outside it. It has also become
clear that increasing amounts of 'fake news' are being spread,
not least during the 2016 presidential campaign in the USA. It is
becoming increasingly important to adopt a critical approach, to
learn to evaluate sources and to seek out supplementary sources.

But your memetic environment doesn't simply consist of things
you see on the internet, but of all kinds of ideas to be found in your
surroundings and which try to enter your consciousness – and

sometimes succeed in doing so. The world is full of ideas. The question is, which ones will you let into your brain? And a still more important issue is how these memes affect your ability to reach your goals and develop in the direction you want. Many memes are useful while others are neutral and still others aren't helpful at all but instead hinder you.

An example of a fairly harmless meme I once heard was about a woman who cut off both ends of the Christmas ham before cooking it. When her friend asked her, "Why do you do that?", she replied, "I don't actually know". "My mother always did that when I was little, but I really have no idea why." So she rang her mother and asked, "Mum, why do we always cut the ends off the Christmas ham?" And her mother laughed uproariously before eventually replying, "It's because when you were a child we only had a really small oven, so the whole ham wouldn't fit!" And as an adult, the daughter had simply carried on doing this without knowing why or questioning whether it made sense – it was simply something that had to be done. You probably have your own similar memes that you've inherited from your family and perhaps never questioned.

And then of course there are memes that are much more serious. These can be memes involving fundamentalism – for example the propaganda that makes young people who have grown up in the West join terrorist organisations in the Middle East. Or the kind of memes that we are exposed to every day, which insist that to be acceptable we must be attractive, thin, fit, successful in our careers, have a perfect home and well-behaved children, the latest fashionable clothes, luxury holidays and loads of friends. Not many of us are able to live up to all of these ideals, with the result that many people are unhappy and feel there's something wrong with them.

One of our culture's norms is that you have to be extroverted and socially active. This is something I tried to live up to for a large part of my life. Despite the fact that I've always been happy being on my own, I felt guilty when I chose to stay in alone on a Friday or Saturday evening. But a few years ago, when I was out in the forest with a good friend and our dogs, I suddenly had an insight. We were talking about how we were both very tired of social activities and about our need for time on our own. And at some point in that conversation, I said, "You know, just because I'm socially competent it doesn't mean that I have any great social needs. Maybe I'm actually an introvert!"

When I came home, I ordered the book *Introvert* by Linus Jonkman (which I warmly recommend, regardless of whether you're an introvert or an extrovert).[38] When I read it, I realised that I recognised myself in much of what it described, and it made me reassess my self-image and accept – and even seek out – my introverted side. When I became conscious that the extrovert norm is actually only a meme, and that I don't have to live up to it, that it's my own choice, I became much more calm and confident as a person. The positive side effect is that I've also become more understanding towards my son, who has always been an introvert. Instead of me nagging him that he should be out meeting his friends, we've now achieved a happy consensus of how nice it is to simply be on your own at home, in peace and quiet. I've also begun to follow a number of blogs and Facebook pages about introversion, and now I'm at the point that I almost think it's cool to be introverted, instead of being ashamed of it like I used to be.

We often inherit memes through our family. The Christmas ham was an example that we can probably all recognise and laugh at. But sometimes memes that we have received from our family can also be obstacles for us. A few years ago I had a coaching client who was extremely intelligent and energetic. She felt under-stimulated and bored in her current job and wanted to move on in her working life. When we discussed and explored what kind of job she was most suited to and would be happiest in, everything pointed to a leading position of some kind, such as a manager or project manager, where she could be influential.

But it turned out that she felt a strong resistance to everything related to careers, advancement and leadership. This was something

---

38 Jonkman (2014)

she had brought with her from her family. Her parents and siblings all had typical blue-collar positions and firmly believed that you shouldn't stand out – that careers were bad and that managers were always representatives of the enemy. When we began to investigate the reasons she felt guilty about her ambitions, it was a very emotional experience for her. She cried bitter tears about how she had adapted herself to her parents' and siblings' values and allowed them to affect her own choices. These values created a strong internal conflict because they prevented her from benefiting from and developing her own primary strengths. When this became clear to her, she decided to break away from the idea that leadership was an evil thing, and not to allow it to hold her back.

Today she is the manager of an entire department and is responsible for 20 employees. She's really happy with her role and is also hugely popular and receives very high scores in employee satisfaction surveys. When I last spoke to her, she said, "Do you know Gunnel, now I feel I'm finally in the right place. I only wish I'd taken this step earlier!"

To manage and discard memes that have taken root and affect you negatively, you first need to become conscious of the ideas or convictions that control your thoughts, choices and actions. The next step is to question them. Is this idea beneficial or harmful for you? Where does it come from? Is there any reason why you should hang onto it? And finally, you can choose not to give it such influence, decide to think differently, choose another conviction. This isn't always easy, particularly with ideas and convictions that you have carried with you for a long time. You may notice that you're slipping back into old thought patterns, but as long as you're conscious of when this happens, you can simply think, "OK, that was the old ideas again" and then say, "But I don't believe them any more".

When you review your memetic environment, reflect upon which sources influence your way of thinking and acting, and consider

whether you can change this, to create optimal conditions for
flourishing and reaching your goals.

REFLECTION: *What does your memetic environment look like?*

- What are the most influential sources of ideas around you just now? These can be newspapers, TV programmes, blogs, internet sites, podcasts, radio programmes, books and other media. They can be your family, friends, celebrities, society, or the culture or religion you belong to.

- Which do you think have the strongest impact on your way of thinking?

- Do they have a positive or negative impact?

Environment no. 8: Body

Your body environment consists of everything related to your body, such as appearance, charisma, health, physical form, weight, stamina and energy, body image, hair, skin, nails and feet. The things you put on, such as clothes, make-up and jewellery, are also part of your body environment. It also includes various professionals who support your physical well-being or help you with your appearance, such as doctors, personal trainers, masseurs, nutritionists, skin therapists and hairdressers.

It can feel strange to see the body as an environment, but it's actually quite logical. You aren't your body. Your body is something you have, and this means you can also affect and 'design' it. The body is also a very important environment because you're in that environment the whole time.

I believe that a positive body image is one of the most important conditions for achieving happiness and well-being. At the same time it's one of the most challenging environments to manage for most people. We can have low self-confidence and think that our bodies are wrong and ugly in every possible way. We are constantly fed almost unachievable ideals about how the perfect body should look. We can have illnesses or disabilities that set limits for us. The most important thing when you look at your body as an environment is to accept and be friends with it, to start from your own circumstances and make the very best of them.

As I mentioned above, your body environment doesn't only consist of your body, but also of everything you put on it. And it has been proven that the characteristics you associate with particular clothes don't merely affect other people's perception of you, but also your own actions. In a study in which the participants were asked to put on a doctor's coat and then carry out certain tasks, it was shown that the doctor's coat made them more attentive and careful.[39] How do you think it affects you if you go to work in baggy jogging bottoms compared to wearing a suit? Of course, this can be very different for different people and also depends on the type of job you have. Regardless of the activity you're going to take part in, you can always improve your own experience of that activity by thinking through the clothes and other attributes that would give you the most self-confidence and would help you to bring out the characteristics you need in that particular situation.

REFLECTION: *What does your own body environment look like?*

– Are you friends with your own body? How well do you look after it?

– Does your body help you in what you want to achieve, or is it instead an obstacle? What can you do to ensure that your body can support you still better in what you want to achieve, on the basis of your own circumstances?

---

39 Adam & Galinsky (2012)

– Do you have clothes, jewellery, a hairstyle and other
attributes that give you self-confidence and help you
to act how you want?

Environment no. 9: Soul

Your soul environment involves everything related to spirituality,
internal harmony, balance, contact with a higher being or a greater
whole, religious practices, meditation, yoga and mindfulness.
In short, how you look after your soul and your psychological
well-being.

Even if you aren't a spiritual person, I hope that you understand
the importance of looking after your soul environment. If you
aren't keen on the word 'soul', you can simply call it your
mental environment.

This is the environment that recharges your batteries and
gives you fuel for achieving the performance you want. It has
a crucial impact on how you feel, your energy level, how alive
you feel and how present you can be. For many of us, the soul
environment is closely linked to nature, which isn't surprising
because nature has so many beneficial effects on us, not least that
it gives us recovery, calmness and harmony. But different people
look after their souls in different ways. Some use meditation,
others go to church or exercise their beliefs in another way. Still
others practice becoming more present in the current moment. A
stressed manager I was coaching once said to me on the subject
of presence, "I'm never present in the current moment. For
example, when I'm doing things with my children, I'm always at
least two steps ahead of where I am and thinking about what I'm
going to do next. It feels like I'm missing my entire life". That
statement provided him with considerable food for thought.

A well-tended soul environment makes you feel good and helps
you experience well-being and happiness. And over the last 15

years, several studies in the area of positive psychology have
demonstrated the effects that happiness, well-being and other
positive emotions have on our performance and on our ability
to achieve our goals. We previously thought it was success that
led to happiness, but research has shown it's actually the opposite
– it's happiness that leads to success. For example, people who
feel positive and happy are more creative, see more opportunities,
find it easy to take in new knowledge and learn new skills, are
better at creating new relationships and achieve better results in
standardised tests. They also have greater resistance to a number
of diseases, recover more quickly from adversity and live longer.
In other words, there are plenty of reasons to take care of your
soul environment.[40]

REFLECTION: *What does your soul environment look like?*

– What do you do to look after your soul and your
psychological well-being?

– Do you have routines and places that help you to relax,
recover, recharge your batteries and find a feeling of
harmony and balance?

– How do you refill yourself with positive emotions?

Environment no. 10: Personality

This environment consists of your character traits, strengths and
weaknesses, talents, skills, values and habits.

Your personality is another environment that you perhaps don't
normally think about as an environment. But it is one, just like
your body. You can develop as a person, utilise and reinforce your
strengths, positive character traits and abilities, and you can find
and emphasise hidden resources. You can remedy your weak-

---

40 See, for example Fredrickson (2011) and Achor (2011)

nesses, question your values and replace limiting beliefs about yourself with more constructive ones. You can change negative patterns, habits and behaviours and replace them with ones that benefit you more. And you can work on your self-confidence.

This largely corresponds to the work you may already have done if you've undergone any form of therapy or coaching, taken personal development courses, listened to inspirational talks or read self-help books. In other words, personal development can be part of the design of your environments.

Just like your body, your personality is an important environment, because you're in it all the time. If you have good levels of self-knowledge, self-esteem and self confidence, are aware of your strengths and weaknesses, can reflect on your own thoughts, values and behaviours, and above all are kind and loving towards yourself, then you naturally have better opportunities for getting where you want than if you are lacking all of this.

One of my best tips for developing this environment is finding out what your main strengths are and trying to use them even more. Many researchers today agree that it is significantly more effective to utilise and build upon your strengths than to remedy weaknesses if you want to achieve genuine success in life.[41] Although of course you should do something about your weaknesses if they get in your way and hinder you. But your weaknesses will never make you a master of anything, so don't spend more energy than necessary on them – it's enough to get them up to a reasonable level. It's by finding and building on your strengths that you can create the best results.

To identify your primary strengths, you can think about what you have always been good at and found easy. But a strength isn't just something you're good at. For example, I'm quite good at admin but it's not one of my strengths because I think it's really boring. Using your strengths gives you energy and flow and makes you feel like your 'real self'. Listen to how you talk about various

---

41 See, for example Linley (2008) and Buckingham & Clifton (2005)

tasks. When you notice that your voice has become exuberant and enthusiastic, you're probably talking about an area where you have a natural strength.

You can also do tests online to find your strengths. One test which has been scientifically developed and taken by over 5 million people across the world – and which is also free – is the *VIA Survey of Character Strengths*. Gallup have also developed a widely used test called *StrengthsFinder*, which you pay a small fee to do. If you search for these names online, you will easily find these tests.

If you don't want to do tests, you can draw up your own 'strength survey'. Send an email to 8-10 people who know you from different contexts – a few colleagues, your manager or perhaps a previous manager, a few family members and a few friends – and ask them to say what they think your primary strengths are. You can also ask about the context or tasks where you are usually at your very best. I often have my coaching clients do this exercise, and it's not only educational but also a real boost for their self-confidence to get as much positive feedback as they usually do.

REFLECTION: *What does your own personality environment look like?*

- Which parts of your personality are you most happy with?

- Which character traits, strengths and talents help you and move you in the right direction? How can you utilise them even better?

- What parts of your personality get in your way and hinder you? How can you manage them?

Summary

As you've seen, pretty much everything you have around you –
and also things within yourself – can be seen as environments.
We have gone through your ten personal environments, seven of
them external and three internal. Your external environments are
the physical environment, your relationships, your networks, your
financial environment, nature, your technological environment and
your memetic environment. Your internal environments are your
body, your soul (or mental environment) and your personality.

You can develop and change all of these environments so that
they become as optimal as possible for you, and so that they give
you support, inspiration and help to move you forwards. In the
next chapter we'll go through the seven steps of this process.

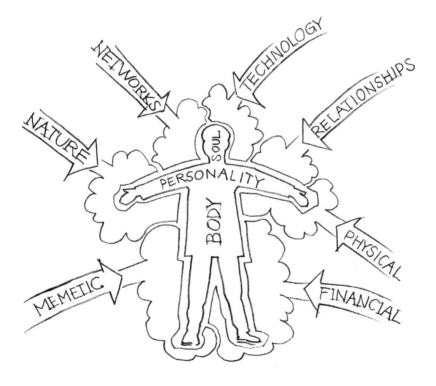

"The first step toward success is taken when you refuse to be a captive of the environment in which you first find yourself."

MARK CAIN

SEVEN STEPS FOR DESIGNING OPTIMAL ENVIRONMENTS

So now you've had an introduction to your 10 environments. Let's now start to look at how you can design them so they help you to achieve your goals and create the life you want. A really optimal environment can make you feel alive. It makes everything feel so much easier and more fun, and helps you to grow and develop in the right direction without having to expend so much of your own willpower and self-discipline.

Designing optimal environments means looking at each of your 10 environments to see what it's like now and what changes you want to make for it to become truly beneficial and to support you in what you want to achieve. This means taking away anything that drains your energy, benefiting from and spending more time on things that give you energy – and adding anything that's missing. It means experimenting with making different changes to see what happens, and perhaps trying out entirely new environments. Sometimes it may not be enough to modify your existing environments – you may discover that you need to completely leave behind one of your existing environments, to change environment or move in some way. Perhaps you need to change job, socialise with different people or move to a new home. When you've reviewed and changed everything you want to change in all of your environments, all you have to do is adapt yourself to your new beneficial environment and allow it to help you move forwards.

In this chapter, I go through seven steps to help you design your own optimal environments. The steps are based on Thomas Leonard's original method, but have also been expanded and adapted, first by Dave Buck and then by me. The order of the steps isn't particularly important, except that step 1 should be first and step 7 last – you can do the others in whichever order you like.

For each step, I've made a list of example changes you can make to each of your 10 environments. But you really should view these lists just as examples. The idea with the lists is simply to clarify the different steps and give you ideas and inspiration – not for you to follow them slavishly. Find the actions and changes you want to make. The most important thing is that you do what's right for you and what gives you the environments you need.

After each step, there are pages where you can review all of your 10 environments, write down your thoughts and plan the changes you want to make to design an ideal environment. At the end of the chapter, there's also a section where you can write down the first steps you want to take, and some pages where you can draw up an overall summary of all the changes you want to implement.

When you review your environments, don't forget to take as the starting point the objectives, dreams and visions that you wrote down in Chapter 4. The whole idea of designing optimal environments is that they should support you to achieve these objectives and visions. So go back and look again at what you wrote in Chapter 4 before you move on.

If you want to take the lazy way to a wonderful life, I recommend that you spend plenty of time now carefully going through each step in each environment. The more willpower you can spend now on doing a thorough review and redesign of your environments, the less dependent you will be on your willpower in the future – and the lazier you can be as a result. In the same way that a wise manager delegates tasks to their employees to free up time and energy, you'll be able to delegate your success to your environments and achieve your objectives without exhausting yourself. View the work you need to do initially as a valuable investment that will give a long-term return.

Step 1: Let your guiding principles be reflected in your environment

In Chapter 4, you thought about your own dreams and objectives. You also formulated guiding principles – short phrases that capture the core of who you want to be and how you want your life to be. Now it's time to see how well your environments live up to your guiding principles.

Look at one environment at a time and compare it with your guiding principles. For example, if one of your phrases is 'lively and happy', can you see 'lively and happy' in your physical environment? Does your physical environment make you feel lively and happy? Or do you instead feel apathetic and unhappy there? What about your relationship environment? Are the people in it lively and happy? Do they make you feel lively and happy?

Look closely at your other environments. How well do they agree with your guiding principles? If you can't see your guiding principles in any environment, think about what you do see. Try to find a few words that summarise the current state of each environment.

Then think about how you can make your environments reflect your guiding principles. What can you change in each of your environments to feel that they all support your guiding principles?

This may feel a bit vague and difficult, but start with small steps and remember that there are no rights or wrongs in this process. Here's an example of how it can work. One of my own guiding principles, which I formulated when I was a teacher at CoachVille, is 'thriving without striving'. It's actually the guiding principle for this entire book! Because thriving without striving is exactly what I wish for you as a reader.

Here are a few things I could do to reflect this guiding principle in each of my environments:

PHYSICAL: Decorate my home so that I am really happy and relaxed when I'm there. Sort out my possessions and fix anything that's broken so that I don't have lots of things around me that drain my energy.

RELATIONSHIPS: Socialise more with a friend who has found a way of thriving without striving – a good role model.

NETWORK: Leave networks, associations or groups that demand too much and stay in or join networks that give a lot and also feel enjoyable.

FINANCIAL: Dare to raise my fee so that I can work less and still cope financially.

NATURE: Always have fresh cut flowers on my kitchen table to remind me of 'thriving'.

TECHNOLOGY: Buy a new, quicker and smaller laptop that's easy to carry in my bag. Use social media to market myself from the comfort of my own sofa.

MEMETIC: Ignore the established idea that you have to make sales calls and customer visits to get bookings. Instead, market myself in ways that I'm happier with, and devote my energy to networking, visibility and doing a really good job that leads to recommendations and follow-up bookings.

BODY: Jog with my dog and do strength training at home – don't feel pressured to go to a gym. Dance more often – it's great exercise that's so much fun that I forget I'm making an effort.

SOUL: Take long walks with my dog in the forest, where I'm present in the current moment and can enjoy the beautiful surroundings and simply being (this brings in the nature environment too – sometimes it's linked with the soul environment).

PERSONALITY: Move my business towards only taking on bookings where I can use my strengths and do what I'm best at.

Step 1: LET YOUR GUIDING PRINCIPLES BE REFLECTED
IN YOUR ENVIRONMENT

My guiding principles (from Chapter 4):

....

....

....

....

....

....

....

Go through your environments one at a time and
answer these questions:

1   How well does this environment correspond to your
       guiding principles? If you can't see your guiding
       principles in this environment, what do you see?
       What words would best summarise the CURRENT
       SITUATION in this environment?

2   Then think about your DESIRED SITUATION.
       What would your ideal environment look like?

3   What can you DO to make this environment
       reflect your guiding principles?

Physical environment

1 *Current situation*...

2 *Desired situation*...

3 *Things to do*...

....

....

Relationships

1 *Current situation*...

2 *Desired situation*...

3 *Things to do*...

....

....

Networks

1 *Current situation*...

2 *Desired situation*...

3 *Things to do*...

....

....

Financial environment

1 *Current situation* ....

2 *Desired situation* ....

3 *Things to do* ....

....

....

Nature

1 *Current situation* ....

2 *Desired situation* ....

3 *Things to do* ....

....

....

Technology

1 *Current situation* ....

2 *Desired situation* ....

3 *Things to do* ....

....

....

Memetic environment

1 *Current situation*..

2 *Desired situation*..

3 *Things to do* ....

....

....

Body

1 *Current situation*..

2 *Desired situation*..

3 *Things to do* ....

....

....

Soul

1 *Current situation*..

2 *Desired situation*..

3 *Things to do* ....

....

....

1 *Current situation*..

2 *Desired situation*..

3 *Things to do* ....

....

....

Step 2: Trash your tolerations

Tolerations are all the things that irritate you, disturb you, distract
you, drain your energy, hinder you, create frustration or delays
in your life or in any other way hold you back. We often talk of
'energy vampires', usually to mean difficult people. 'Tolerations'
is a broader concept that I've borrowed directly from Thomas
Leonard. He defines them as the things you tolerate in your
environment but which actually drain you and are more harmful
than helpful to you. He says that we should try to strive to become
'toleration-free zones' – in other words, to remove all tolerations
from our lives. Tolerations needn't only be things that irritate
you – they can also be things that prevent you from acting as you
want and that support 'incorrect' behaviour. For example having
a house full of sweets when you've decided to eat healthily.

    Tolerations can be both large and small. Often it isn't the big
catastrophic things that are the worst, but all the small things
that gradually add up, eventually taking too much of the energy
that you could otherwise have spent on more enjoyable or more
productive activities.

EXAMPLES of tolerations are:

- *Disorder and mess*
- *Things that are broken or incomplete – for example a house that you never finish renovating*
- *Negative relationships*
- *Family members who ridicule your dreams*
- *Friends who constantly complain about everything*
- *Information overload*
- *Exhausting thoughts and beliefs*
- *Low energy levels*
- *A long to-do list*
- *A lack of reserves (financial, emotional, mental, physical)*
- *Absolutely anything a person can complain about*

Tolerations drain energy. The bigger and more numerous they are, the more they drain us. So it's a good idea to try to get rid of them and quite simply clean up your environments.

How do you do that? To begin with, you should try to **ELIMINATE** the toleration so that you get rid of it completely. Eliminating a toleration involves taking action, changing the situation, removing the obstacle or no longer spending time on the toleration.

Here are a few EXAMPLES of how you can eliminate tolerations in your different environments:

PHYSICAL: Deal with your backlog, sort out your paperwork, clean out your wardrobe and other storage and donate or discard clothes and things you haven't used for several years, repaint the wall that's been annoying you for so long, repair anything that's broken or fix anything that's draining your energy.

RELATIONSHIPS: Stop socialising with people who drain your energy.

NETWORK: Leave any club or association that takes more energy than it gives.

FINANCIAL: Get rid of unnecessary expenses.

NATURE: Cut down a tree that's blocking out the sun or the view in your garden.

TECHNOLOGY: Decide to switch off your mobile phone after dinner every evening or shut down your social media accounts if you think they're preventing you from focusing on what you actually want to do.

MEMETIC: Stop reading a blog that only makes you feel inferior.

BODY: Get rid of the excess weight so that you can do more. Stop eating sweets, stop smoking or drinking alcohol.

SOUL: Spend less time in environments that stress you.

PERSONALITY: Decide to stop thinking negative thoughts about yourself. Remedy a weakness that's holding you back in some way.

Whatever tolerations you choose to eliminate and however you choose to do it, I guarantee that it will affect how you feel. You will almost certainly be relieved, feel better, think more clearly and find it easier to focus on what you want to achieve.

Of course, it's not always so easy to completely eliminate a toleration. Particularly not if it's a person close to you – perhaps your partner or a good friend – who's irritating you. Perhaps you don't want to eliminate them at all. You can undoubtedly change both partner and friends, but perhaps they have good sides too, that you really want to keep.

Just because somebody is to some extent a toleration doesn't mean that you have to completely remove them from your life. But you need to think about how you can change your relationship to eliminate the aspect that disturbs you. Perhaps by standing up for yourself and your needs more, communicating more clearly and more honestly and saying what you want from the other person. Often tolerations in relationships involve promises and expectations that haven't been fulfilled and things that haven't been explicitly stated. These can frequently be dealt with through clear communication.

For example, you might have lent money to a friend who hasn't paid you back. Every time you meet, it annoys you that they don't even mention the money, and this drains your energy. Tell the person straight out that you want your money back. For example, say: "I really appreciate you as a friend, but I've been getting irritated recently that you haven't repaid me the money I lent you. I'd like you to pay back the loan as soon as you can so that it isn't causing friction in our relationship".

There are some things in your environment that you can't affect at all – such as a chronic illness, the economic situation or the weather. There may also be things that you can't do anything about just now, perhaps because your finances limit your opportunities to act. Where you can't eliminate a toleration, you have to adopt the second strategy and **ACCEPT** it. If you can't get rid of it, you must instead try to change your own attitude. This doesn't mean that you continue to put up with the toleration, but instead that you truly accept it and no longer permit it to drain as much energy from you. This needn't mean that you like it, but instead that it can no longer exhaust you.

The first step to doing this is awareness. Tolerations are products of our thoughts. It isn't the situation itself that drains your energy, but instead your reaction to the situation. For example, take a messy kitchen. One person might be driven mad by it, while another might think it was completely fine. In other words, it isn't the messy kitchen in itself, but instead our thoughts about it that determine whether or not it's a toleration.

So how can you change your thoughts? Well, by increasing your awareness and deciding to change them.

"If you don't like something, change it. If you can't change it, change your attitude."

MAYA ANGELOU

Let me give you an example. Several years ago I and my then husband bought a house that needed a lot of renovation. We did a thorough job of it – we did some of the work ourselves but much of it was done by a building company. Gradually the money ran out. By that stage almost everything was done. Pretty much all that was left was the final pieces of trim. Skirting boards, ceiling mouldings, window and door trim. For a full six months I went round being annoyed by the missing pieces of trim. I was so frustrated by this detail, and it drained so much of my energy, that I found it difficult to relax and enjoy our home. This is actually incredibly ironic and really rather ridiculous because we now had a beautiful house where everything was in great condition and exactly how we wanted it. We'd redesigned the layout so that it suited us, I was really happy with our material and colour choices and it was actually perfect. 95% of the house was done, but of course I focused on the final 5% that wasn't finished.

When I became aware of what I was doing and how much I was allowing my thoughts to control how I felt, I decided to change my focus. I was going to stop being irritated about the trim, accept that the house was going to look like this for a while and focus on everything we'd actually achieved. In other words, the first step was acceptance. I also talked to my husband and together we drew up a strategy for finishing everything within six months. We were both incredibly busy at the time, and I'm all thumbs when it comes to DIY, so we planned to save some money every month so that before Christmas we would be able to afford to get the building company to install all of the missing pieces of trim – thereby completely eliminating the toleration. As soon as this was agreed, it also became easier to let go of my irritation.

Why don't we all get rid of our tolerations? Tolerations are tricky things. They are often associated with an obvious cost. What's less obvious is that we often also gain some kind of benefit from them. So we need to understand both the cost and benefit of keeping the toleration. It's also true that every change has a price, and we aren't always willing to pay it. So in other words we don't always want to pay the price for eliminating the toleration. Every time we weigh up the change, we compare cost against benefit – sometimes consciously and sometimes unconsciously.

Here are a few EXAMPLES of how a toleration can also have a kind of perceived 'benefit' – that is, a reason not to do away with it.

– *Someone can be very tired of their partner, but if that partner brings in the majority of the household's income, that can be a reason to remain in the relationship.*

– *Some people enjoy being martyrs, feeling sorry for themselves and hoping to get other people's sympathy – and perhaps being able to whinge and complain to their friends as well. If they trash their tolerations so that they have no complaints left, what will they talk about?*

– *It can also be a question of self-righteousness – a desire to show what a good person you are and how exploited you are by everybody who wants your help (this is a variation of the martyr).*

– *One common reason for hanging onto your tolerations is, of course, that you feel secure in what's familiar, that change requires a lot of energy and a feeling of 'better the devil you know'. In other words, it's better to stay in a rather boring job than risk the next job being even worse. Or perhaps even being unemployed.*

— *By hanging onto what is and avoiding change, you also*
avoid exposing yourself to the risk of failure. Imagine if I
chase my dream and then don't achieve it, and everyone
in my family says, "You should have listened to me", and
I don't bring in any money and have to sell the flat, and the
kids have to live on instant noodles.

I'm sure you have your own examples of tolerations that for one
reason or another you choose to keep. The most important thing is
to try to be aware of your motives, and if you keep a toleration,
try to find a way that you can also accept it so that you don't allow
it to drain or hinder you.

NOW IT'S YOUR TURN!
Step 2: TRASH YOUR TOLERATIONS

1   What OBSTACLES AND TOLERATIONS do you have
       in your environments? Do you have any tolerations that
       you keep purely out of habit or comfort, despite the fact
       that you'd feel better if you got rid of them?

2   How can you trash your tolerations? Which ones can you
       completely ELIMINATE, and which ones do you need to
       find ways to ACCEPT?

Physical environment

1 *Tolerations/obstacles* ....

....

2 *How to eliminate/accept*

....

....

Relationships

1 *Tolerations/obstacles* ....

....

2 *How to eliminate/accept*

....

....

Networks

1 *Tolerations/obstacles* ....

....

2 *How to eliminate/accept*

....

....

Financial environment

1 *Tolerations/obstacles* ....

....

2 *How to eliminate/accept*

....

....

1 *Tolerations/obstacles* ....

....

2 *How to eliminate/accept*

....

....

Technology

1 *Tolerations/obstacles* ....

....

2 *How to eliminate/accept*

....

....

Memetic environment

1 *Tolerations/obstacles* ....

....

2 *How to eliminate/accept*

....

....

Body

1 *Tolerations/obstacles* ....

....

2 *How to eliminate/accept*

....

....

Soul

1 *Tolerations/obstacles* ....

....

2 *How to eliminate/accept*

....

....

Personality

1 *Tolerations/obstacles* ....

....

2 *How to eliminate/accept*

....

....

Step 3: Cultivate your resources

Simply getting rid of your tolerations isn't enough to create a fantastic environment – it merely turns it from poor to acceptable. If you want an optimal environment, you also need to highlight and utilise the things that are already good. Resources are all the things in your environment that inspire you, fill you with energy, support you, make you feel good, make you believe in yourself, help you move forwards or challenge you in a positive way.

EXAMPLES of resources are:

- *Things that are clearly visible and easily accessible in your physical environment that remind you of your ambitions and make it easy for you to stick to them*
- *Tools and technical aids that work well, or an app that you couldn't manage without*
- *Positive relationships, family and friends who believe in and support you*
- *A good network, role models who can inspire you and people who have ambitions, interests or dreams similar to yours*
- *A pleasant and harmonious home*
- *Inspiring books, websites, newspapers, blogs and podcasts*
- *Awareness of your own talents and strengths*
- *Mental harmony and balance*
- *Routines and structures that create order*
- *Ordered finances*
- *A favourite place in nature that gives you peace and revitalises you*
- *A mentor or coach*
- *Routines for regularly looking after yourself, both physically and mentally*
- *Anything that makes you feel full of life*

Resources can be both things that give you support and things that give you healthy challenges and make you strive that little bit further. But remember that there's a difference between challenges and obstacles. Challenges help you to develop and be better. Obstacles are in the way and cause unnecessary problems. If you play football and are trying to score, and a player in the opposing team is trying to stop you, that's a challenge because it's helping you to become a better player. But if you're playing football and there's a big hole in the pitch that you have to avoid so you don't break an ankle, that's an unnecessary obstacle because it can only injure you.

When you're thinking about the resources you need for your environment to give you optimal conditions for development in the direction you want, you can compare yourself with an athlete who wants to be really good at their sport. Some things you might need could be:

- *Other people who do the kind of thing you want to develop, both those on your own level and those who are on a higher level*
- *Challenges that make you give a little bit extra to get really good*
- *Support when you're feeling down*
- *Lots of opportunities to practice what you want to improve*

One of my primary resources when it comes to my professional development as a speaker is the National Speakers Association of Sweden, which was formed a few years ago. Running my own company as a speaker is quite a solitary job – everything hangs on me. So having access to a network with more than 100 colleagues I can be inspired by and learn from, exchange ideas and experiences with, is enormously valuable to me. You might think that professional speakers are prone to playing the diva, that we have big egos and are incredibly competitive with each other. Perhaps some divas do exist. But in any case there aren't any in our association. I don't think I've ever experienced such generosity and openness as I have in this group. Everyone's equally happy to have found like-minded colleagues and we lavishly share our experiences, support each other, give each other tips about jobs, collaborate on a range of assignments and projects, and discuss everything under the sun. We have skills development events on various themes and invite each other to listen to and give feedback on our talks. The speakers association has quite simply become a fantastic resource in my environment, and I try to take part in as many activities as I can, both in-person with our physical meetings and online in our discussion forum.

The most important thing of all when we talk about resources is perhaps our very closest relationships. Growing and developing isn't a solo project, and nobody can achieve their full potential in isolation. To genuinely flourish, we need warm, trusting relation-ships with other people, regardless of whether they're life partners, family, close friends or colleagues. Psychiatrist George Valliant discovered that people who have someone in their life that they'd be comfortable ringing at 4 am to talk about their worries with are happier and live longer than those who lack such a person.[42]

My sister Ingrid is this kind of resource for me. And she's now very close at hand, because we bought a house together two years ago. I had been divorced for a few years and my sister was recently widowed, so we decided to buy a two-family house where we each have our own space, both for company and so that we can help each other out with practical things. This has been a great solution for both of us, and the best thing is that we've gone from simply being sisters to also being each other's best friend and support. As well as encouraging and always believing in me, my sister also contributes to making my life enormously easier by looking after my dog when I'm out travelling for work.

And of course resources needn't necessarily just be people. Resources can be present in all of your environments, and can

42 Seligman (2012)

be everything from things and places to routines and sources of ideas and knowledge. For example, all of my books are important resources from which I gather knowledge and inspiration for my own writing and my talks. The house I share with my sister, which I absolutely love, is another resource, and our garden, where I relax by doing physical tasks, is yet another.

For many people, nature is an important resource. My sister once described how, while out in the forest walking the dogs, she spotted a man standing completely still under a tree, a little way from the path. He was holding something in one hand, and to begin with she thought it was a pair of binoculars, so she asked if he was watching birds. He smiled and replied, "No, I'm just taking everything in", and my sister saw that he was actually holding a coffee cup. He was just standing there breathing, drinking coffee and observing and absorbing everything beautiful in the forest. Doesn't that sound wonderful? He had really understood the concept of 'forest bathing'.

Once you've identified the resources you already have in your environments, you really need to utilise them. Think about how you can cultivate your resources, get them to grow, build further on them or spend more time with them.

Here are just a few EXAMPLES of how you can cultivate and utilise resources in your different environments.

PHYSICAL: Think of the physical environment you're happiest in and where you feel full of life. Perhaps you have a special place in your home where you can really relax, or a summer home, or a caravan you love being in. Think about what it's like at work. Perhaps there's a place there that helps you to be extra creative and effective. Spend more time in the places where you feel and function best.

RELATIONSHIPS: Identify the friends who really make you feel good and spend more time with them.

NETWORK: Invite someone from your network who inspires you out for lunch.

FINANCIAL: Book time for a financial advice session with your bank contact. Resume a routine you've previously found useful for managing and keeping track of your finances, such as a household budget or keeping accounts of your income and outgoings to see what you're spending money on. Be more active in choosing how your pension savings are invested.

NATURE: Do you have a favourite place outdoors, somewhere you feel calm and harmonious? Go there more often and simply sit, or stand, for a little while and enjoy it. Your natural environment includes pets too. If you have a dog, cat or other pet, look after it and spend more time with it. Spending time with animals is very good for your well-being.

TECHNOLOGY: Learn more about your technical aids. Read up on and find functions that you haven't previously tried but can help you to get even more benefit, for example from your computer, mobile phone or digital camera.

MEMETIC: Spend time every evening reading a chapter of an interesting book. Spend more time following blogs and podcasts that you find inspiring.

BODY: If you've found a good masseur, personal trainer, skin therapist or someone else who helps you with your body, your physical well-being or appearance – treat yourself and book regular visits to them.

SOUL: Think about what you've already tried that helps you to find balance and calm. Perhaps you have a mindfulness course that you enjoyed but that you haven't listened to for a while. Maybe you once learned a relaxation exercise that you found useful but have stopped doing. Or perhaps you find calmness in nature.

Resume whatever you know works for you. If you already meditate every morning and feel wonderful for doing so, consider meditating for a little longer, or even doing a session in the afternoon or evening too. Simply do more of what makes you feel good.

PERSONALITY: Utilise your strengths. If you don't already know what your primary strengths are, find out (see the tips in Chapter 5, Environment no. 10). Use your strengths as much as you can. And try to find new situations where you can benefit from them. Talk about your strengths to your manager and suggest ways you can use and develop them more.

NOW IT'S YOUR TURN!
Step 3: CULTIVATE YOUR RESOURCES

1   What RESOURCES do you have in your environments?

2   How can you GET EVEN MORE BENEFIT from them?

Physical environment

1 *Resources* ....

....

2 *More benefit* ....

....

Relationships

1 *Resources* ....

....

2 *More benefit*

Networks

1 *Resources*

2 *More benefit*

Financial environment

1 *Resources*

2 *More benefit*

Nature

1 *Resources*

2 *More benefit*

Technology

1 *Resources* ....

....

2 *More benefit* ....

....

Memetic environment

1 *Resources* ....

....

2 *More benefit* ....

....

Body

1 *Resources* ....

....

2 *More benefit* ....

....

Soul

1 *Resources* ....

....

....

Personality

1 *Resources* ....

....

2 *More benefit* ....

....

Step 4: Add what's missing

In addition to the resources you already have, you may discover you want to add something that's missing from your current environments. This step is about identifying the additional resources you'd like to have so you can create truly optimal environments. Think about what could give you even more inspiration and energy. What would make you feel good and give you impetus so that you can more easily get where you want? This could be people, places, things, habits, influences or perhaps some quality or skill in yourself.

When I started my own company, I realised quite quickly that I wasn't socialising with other self-employed people, and I was missing someone to exchange ideas and experience with and to get tips and inspiration from. So I began actively seeking out different business networks and opportunities to meet other entrepreneurs; lots of interesting people I could exchange business cards and arrange lunches with so that we could get to know each other better. I also contacted acquaintances who I knew ran their own businesses, and started meeting them more regularly. This made a big difference for me during my first few years of self-employment. It gave me support, inspiration and people to bounce ideas off.

I added my dog Nalle to my natural environment nearly ten years ago. At that time I'd just started my own company after being on sick leave with burnout for six months. I grew up with dogs and have always loved them, but getting one this time was also a way to make sure that I'd never again fall into the trap of working too much. With a dog I was more or less forced to work shorter days and take breaks, and to go out on regular walks in the fresh air. A perfect countermeasure against stress. I also got exercise, love, lots of fun and a best friend into the bargain. And in fact, Nalle isn't just part of my natural environment, but also of my soul environment, my relationship environment... and even my body environment because he makes sure I get exercise.

In the physical environment it can be quite easy to come up with things you want to add. But try not to acquire lots of gadgets simply because your friends have them. Instead make sure they're things that actually can make a difference to you and which will support you in what you want to achieve. For example a bicycle if you've decided to exercise more and want to start cycling to work. Or a hammock if you want to practice being lazier.

You can also add a physical symbol of some type that reminds you of your goals. One manager I coached had problems capturing all the 'balls' that his employees threw at him, and took it upon himself to solve all the problems instead of throwing them back and coaching the employees to solve the problems themselves. He decided to keep a tennis ball clearly visible on his desk to remind himself about his goals and that he needed to throw more balls back.

Think about what's missing from your own environments. If you reflect for a while, I'm sure you can come up with a long wish list. Perhaps you can't add everything at once, particularly if they're things that cost money. But you can try adding one or more of the things you want at a time.

Here are a few EXAMPLES of things you could add to your different environments:

PHYSICAL: Buy a new lawn mower (I've just replaced my old manual one with a battery-powered lawn mower – and what a difference! It's suddenly become a pleasure to cut the grass.) Replace your old sofa with a new one, hang up new curtains, pictures of your family, friends, sports team or something else that helps you enjoy your home more. If your goal is to eat more healthily, perhaps you want to invest in a kitchen appliance that will help you to do so – a juicer, a mixer or a spiraliser. If it's also attractive and you have it out on the kitchen counter, it isn't just a tool but also a reminder about your new healthy you, making it easy for you to do what you've decided to.

RELATIONSHIPS: Think about the people you're already acquainted with. Are there any you'd like to get to know better and socialise with more? Perhaps someone who has similar goals, interests and ambitions as you.

NETWORK: Join a network for people with the same profession or interests as you. Join an interesting group on LinkedIn. Register for a course, join an association or find some other form of meeting place where you can find inspiring people.

FINANCIAL: Open a savings or share dealing account and start saving monthly. Book time with a financial or pension advisor. If you're self-employed like me, find an accountant so you can spend more time on your own core business. Download an app that will help you draw up a household budget and keep track of your income and expenses.

NATURE: Start growing something – anything. It could be your own vegetable plot if you have a garden, cherry tomatoes on the balcony or herbs in your kitchen window. Get a pet.

TECHNOLOGY: Buy a new, faster computer or some other technical gadget that makes it easier to achieve what you want –

or that's just more fun. If you want to be more effective, download apps that give you better structure and help you organise your work. You can also get apps that encourage you to exercise, meditate, cook exciting new dishes or whatever you want to do.

MEMETIC: Find new influences and sources of ideas, information and knowledge within an area that can move you closer to what you want to achieve. This could be something like podcasts, books, radio programmes or blogs.

BODY: If your goal is to get into better shape, find a training partner who'll ring your doorbell at an agreed time – this makes it difficult to come up with excuses. Or buy a bicycle and leave it easily accessible while you lock your car in the garage and hide the key.

SOUL: Create your own morning routine that gives you a good start to the day. Buy a notebook that you write a few thoughts in every evening, for example about the day that has passed, any lessons you have learned, what went well and what you're looking forward to in the morning.

PERSONALITY: Go on a personal development course. Read a self-help book. Challenge yourself to do something you've never done before.

And here's a bonus tip for anyone who's single and wants their environment to help them find a partner: researchers have shown that by choosing to be present in a particular type of environment, you can affect other people's feelings and behaviours. One example is that a warm environment encourages warmer behaviour, while a cold environment leads to colder behaviour.[43] So next time you're going on a date with a potential partner, make sure you're in a warm environment – or offer them a hot drink, as this can also work.

---

43 IJzerman & Semin (2009)

Another trick you can try out is to do something exciting – perhaps even something a little bit scary – with your date. A physical energy boost, for example from a trip on a rollercoaster, makes your date think that you're more attractive than you actually are. The rush in their body can even make the other person feel that they are in love with you. And you can have the same effect if you give your date an energy drink.[44] Perhaps something worth trying?

NOW IT'S YOUR TURN!
Step 4: ADD WHAT'S MISSING

What would you like to ADD to your environments that could give you even more energy, inspiration and impetus?

Physical environment

....

....

....

44 Dutton & Aron (1974)

130 *Relationships* ....

....

....

....

Networks ....

....

....

Financial environment ....

....

....

Nature ....

....

....

Technology ....

....

....

Body ....

Soul ....

Personality ....

Step 5: Experiment with your existing environments

The fifth step involves experimenting with changes, just to see if they make any difference. Here it's all about making changes in your existing environments – in other words, the environments you already have around you and feel at home in. In the next stage, we'll take the step outside your familiar environments and try out completely new ones.

Experimenting means manipulating your environments with a child's curiosity and playfulness. Try removing or adding something, moving things or behaving differently and see how this feels and how it affects you. The whole idea of experimenting is that you don't have to stick with the change. Simply try it out and see what happens. If it doesn't work you can always change it back. Use this step to try out things that you still haven't quite decided about yet.

Here are a few EXAMPLES of experiments for your different environments:

PHYSICAL ENVIRONMENT: Change your furniture, move your desk or your bed, replace a picture, add something clearly visible that can symbolise your goal so that you're constantly reminded of it.

RELATIONSHIPS: Try behaving differently towards someone close to you. For example, be clearer with what you need, want or expect from your relationship. Say 'No' to something you'd otherwise normally say 'Yes' to. Or vice versa. Say 'Yes' a little more often if you normally say 'No'.

NETWORK: Try adopting a different role than you usually do in a network you're already part of. Perhaps take on more – and take up more space. Contact someone in your network who inspires you and bounce ideas off them or ask for advice.

FINANCIAL: Write down everything you buy for a month to get a clearer image of what you're spending your money on.

NATURE: Go outdoors for a little while every lunchtime for a week. Even if you're in a town, you can go and sit under a tree, visit a park or watch pigeons in the square.

TECHNOLOGY: Learn more about your email program and the functions that can help you to become more effective, be more active on LinkedIn, or on the contrary abstain from social media for a week.

MEMETIC: Read a different daily newspaper than you normally do every day for a week. Reflect on your habits and routines. Where do they come from and can you try doing something differently? Choose not to take in information from sources that you normally follow but that only drag you down.

BODY: Decide to change your eating habits or walk for 30 minutes a day for a week. Use your physical environment as an aid – for example by filling up your refrigerator and pantry with food that you want to eat and hiding things you don't want to eat, by putting out your most comfortable walking shoes, setting an alarm on your mobile for the time you want to walk and downloading audiobooks you've been meaning to get around to so you can listen to them as you walk.

SOUL: Borrow a CD with relaxation exercises from the library and try out doing one exercise every day for a week.

PERSONALITY: Suggest to your manager that you could work in another department for a little while or try out some completely new tasks where you can use and develop your strengths.

NOW IT'S YOUR TURN!

Step 5: EXPERIMENT WITH YOUR EXISTING
ENVIRONMENTS

What can you EXPERIMENT WITH in your existing environments? Is there something you can TEST just to see how it feels?

Physical environment..

....

....

....

....

Relationships..

....

....

....

....

Networks...

....

....

....

....

Financial environment ....

....

....

....

....

Nature ....

....

....

....

Technology ....

....

....

....

Memetic environment ....

....

....

....

....

Body ....

....

....

....

....

Soul ....

....

....

....

....

Personality ....

....

....

....

....

Step 6: Try out entirely new environments

The previous step, experimenting with your existing environments, means that you try out something new in an environment you're already familiar with and feel at home in. Trying out entirely new environments is a bigger step, as you move outside your habitual, safe and comfortable environments and try out a new, unknown environment.

Try it out and see how it feels! Just like when you experiment, you don't need to stick with the new environments (even if some things can be difficult to back out of immediately, for example if you move house or change job).

Sometimes it can be difficult to draw a clear boundary between experimenting in existing environments and trying out completely new ones. These two steps can to some extent run into each other, depending on how you interpret what an existing environment and what a new one are. But it isn't so important that you have a clear definition or boundary. The most important thing is that you think about the changes you'll experiment with and try to come up with both small and large changes.

Some EXAMPLES of trying out new environments:

PHYSICAL ENVIRONMENT: Move to a new home. Change job. Buy a caravan or a boat, or rent a mobile home or a holiday cottage.

RELATIONSHIPS: Register on an internet dating site. Join a singles club or another organisation where you can meet new friends. Register for a study circle or course where you can meet new people.

NETWORK: Go along as a guest to a professional business network such as BNI or Rotary.

FINANCIAL: Go on a course in stock market investment. Book time with an insurance adviser. Find an extra job.

NATURE: Find new ways of getting into contact with nature. Perhaps learn to ride, sail or cycle. Get an allotment and start to grow your own vegetables. Sit outdoors and work a few hours a day or take your work colleagues on a walking meeting outside instead of sitting in a conference room.

TECHNOLOGY: Buy a new mobile phone, tablet or computer. Learn to use a new app or a new computer program that can help you to feel better or be more effective. Find a new virtual meeting place where you can interact with other people.

MEMETIC: Read books on a totally new subject. Break an old tradition or cultural norm that's holding you back rather than helping you. Find an inspiring new information source.

BODY: Go along with a good friend to their gym or dance course. Become vegetarian.

SOUL: Try going to an opera or dance performance, read poetry, or something else that can contribute to mental well-being and that you haven't tried out before.

PERSONALITY: Start a course, learn something you didn't know before. Then change your old environment so that it supports your 'new' you. Go to a coach or therapist.

NOW IT'S YOUR TURN!
Step 6: TRY OUT ENTIRELY NEW ENVIRONMENTS

Would you like to try out an ENTIRELY NEW ENVIRONMENT? If so, which?

Physical environment..

....

....

....

....

Networks ....

....

....

Financial environment ....

....

....

Nature ....

....

....

Technology ....

....

....

Memetic environment ....

....

....

Body ....

....

....

Soul ....

....

....

Personality ....

....

....

Step 7: Adapt to your environments

Now you've gone through all of your environments and reviewed the changes you want to make. You've thought about how you can let your guiding principles be reflected in your environments, the tolerations you have and how you can either eliminate or accept them, the resources you have and how you can get even more benefit from them, and what you're lacking in your environments that you could add to get even more support, inspiration and impetus. You've perhaps already found some experiments you can try in your existing environments, and you may have also already come up with some entirely new ones that you want to try out. Congratulations. If you've written down your ideas, you now have a complete action plan for designing your new environments!

Once you've gone through all of your environments and made all the changes you want to make, so that they give you maximum support, inspiration and energy and help you move in the right direction, there's only one thing left to do – adapt yourself to your upgraded environments and allow them to help you move forwards. In this step, you don't need to do anything yourself – you simply harvest the fruit of the work you did in steps 1-6.

If you have really succeeded in designing beneficial environments, you'll soon notice that you feel inspired, alive and full of energy, that you're growing and developing in the right direction, that life feels a little bit more how you want it to be and that everything feels much easier and more fun because you won't need to rely only on your own self discipline and willpower. The environment will help you to move towards your goals, just as if you were sitting at the top of the slide I wrote about in the introduction, with your goal at the bottom.

All you need to do is enjoy the ride.

To do straight away

To truly move from words to action and achieve changes in your environment, use what you've written down in this chapter as your action plan. Decide on A FIRST STEP for each environment – something you can do almost immediately. You don't need to put all your ideas into practice at once. Take one thing at a time and prioritise your ideas. Because you know the best way to eat an elephant, don't you? One bite at a time! When you've finished your first step, you can come back to what you wrote and choose which step to take next. And you can add any new ideas that come to mind. And in the end, you'll have eaten the entire elephant and designed really good environments for yourself to grow and flourish in.

Physical environment..

....

....

Relationships ....

....

....

Networks ....

....

....

Financial environment ....

....

....

Nature ....

....

....

Technology ....

....

....

....

Memetic environment ....

....

....

Body ....

....

....

Soul ....

....

....

Personality ....

....

....

On the following pages you can, if you want, summarise the things you've come up with in this chapter so that you have an overview of the most important changes you want to make to your environments. After that, we'll leave your ten personal environments and go over to the environment you share with your colleagues – your working environment.

OVERVIEW – *my notes*

PHYSICAL ENVIRONMENT

1. Guiding principles ....

2. Tolerations ....

3. Resources ....

4. Missing ....

5. Experiment ....

6. New environment ....

First step ....

RELATIONSHIPS

1. Guiding principles ....

2. Tolerations ....

3. Resources ....

4. Missing ....

5. Experiment ....

6. New environment ....

First step ....

NETWORKS

1. Guiding principles ....

2. Tolerations ....

3. Resources ....

4. Missing ....

5. Experiment ....

6. New environment ....

First step ....

FINANCIAL ENVIRONMENT

1. Guiding principles ....

2. Tolerations ....

3. Resources ....

4. Missing ....

5. Experiment ....

6. New environment ....

First step ....

1. Guiding principles

2. Tolerations

3. Resources

4. Missing

5. Experiment

6. New environment

First step

TECHNOLOGY

1. Guiding principles

2. Tolerations

3. Resources

4. Missing

5. Experiment

6. New environment

First step

MEMETIC ENVIRONMENT

1. Guiding principles ....

2. Tolerations ....

3. Resources ....

4. Missing ....

5. Experiment ....

6. New environment ....

First step ....

BODY

1. Guiding principles ....

2. Tolerations ....

3. Resources ....

4. Missing ....

5. Experiment ....

6. New environment ....

First step ....

1. Guiding principles ....

2. Tolerations ....

3. Resources ....

4. Missing ....

5. Experiment ....

6. New environment ....

First step ....

PERSONALITY

1. Guiding principles ....

2. Tolerations ....

3. Resources ....

4. Missing ....

5. Experiment ....

6. New environment ....

First step ....

PART 3:

OPTIMISE YOUR WORKING ENVIRONMENT

"We are each other's environment — we make each other better!"

PIA SUNDHAGE

YOUR WORKING ENVIRONMENT

In Part Two, we primarily focused on your own, personal ten environments and how you can upgrade them. The majority of these ten environments are represented both in your leisure time and at work. For example, at work you have aspects of your physical, relationship, network, memetic and technological environments. Your personality environment, with your talents and strengths, is hopefully nourished by your work. Your financial environment is also strongly linked to your employment. If you've read Part Two and thought about the changes you want to make in your ten environments, I'm sure you've already reflected quite a bit on your working environment.

Here in Part Three we'll be taking a closer look at your working environment. The majority of us spend a large proportion of our time at work, and it's also where we strive to achieve many of our goals. So it can be valuable to look more closely at your working environment. Another reason why I've chosen to give this particular environment a separate section of the book is that it's an environment that most of us share with other people. And this means that when it comes to the working environment you can't simply act on the basis of yourself and how YOU want to design your environments. You and your colleagues also need to take each other's desires into account and to combine and adapt your various needs and wishes about how you ALL want your shared environment to be.

You're also all part of each other's working environment, which means that you each need to look at yourself and consider how you can be as good an environment as possible for your colleagues. This naturally also applies outside work – you form part of other people's environment in your leisure time too, so you need to think about what it's like to have you as part of that environment, and try to be a resource for your family, your friends and your network.

In this chapter I give you tips and ideas about how you and your colleagues can work together to create a working environment that draws you in the right direction and helps you to flourish, be happy, feel job satisfaction, perform better, develop and achieve great results. An environment that makes it easy to feel good and succeed.

And I'd like to emphasise that you don't need to be a manager to benefit from this part of the book. You may think your working environment is primarily your manager's responsibility, but this is really aimed at anyone who works in any way. There are lots of things we can all do to help create a really good environment for ourselves and our colleagues.

Are you inspired or drained at work?

Perhaps, like me, you've been in workplaces with very different working environments. Just like other environments, the working environment can make it easy for us to feel good, develop, perform better and achieve good results, or it can hinder us and hold us back. Some environments help us to flourish, while others make us wither. Let me tell you about two really different workplaces I've found myself in.

In the late 1990s I got a job as a project manager for an employment market course run by a major training company. During the job interview process, I formed an image of an exciting role in an organisation that kept a close eye on the latest educational research and was at the cutting edge when it came to transforming that research into practical work. There was a great deal of focus on providing a creative and inspiring learning environment for the course participants. Because I had a degree in education, I naturally thought this sounded really exciting.

But when I started with the company I quickly realised that all these new, modern ideas hadn't actually reached the subsidiary where I was going to work. My workplace was a grey concrete colossus from the 1970s. And it wasn't merely the building that was grey and heavy, but the entire culture. The atmosphere was negative and grudging and the grumpy men who'd worked there since the building was constructed called any new idea about changing the environment 'female nonsense' and 'piffle'. Of course, I'm fully aware that women can also be negative and irritable, but in this particular workplace the men were in the majority. It was 1999, but the office looked exactly as it must have done in 1970. It was so boring and uninspiring that I couldn't see how anyone could stand working there. And yet there was absolutely no comprehension of the fact that change might improve it. When one of the 'old guard' one day discovered that my colleague and I had hung up new curtains and paintings and had also brought in some branches and twigs from the forest for decoration, he grumbled at every break for more than a week about how stupid it all was – and the other guys all agreed with him.

Apart from the generally negative atmosphere, it also turned out that my office was a dark little space without windows and that my tasks could actually have been done by pretty much anyone. They could have just picked up anyone from the street. My education and experience were totally unnecessary. I don't think I've ever felt so under-stimulated, and there was absolutely no way of utilising my strengths or developing my skills.

Fortunately I was pregnant when I got the job, so after six months I could go on parental leave. Then I made sure I got another job, and this one was a complete contrast to the previous one.

I was employed as a business coordinator in a major redeployment project. We built up an organisation of 50 employees from scratch and ran it for two years, helping almost 1000 people to obtain new employment. And then we closed it all down when the project was over.

The atmosphere in this workplace was completely different. On one occasion, one of my colleagues said that the atmosphere could be described as 50% professionalism and 50% madness. It was happy and enthusiastic, but at the same time everyone was extremely professional. There was a strong sense of cohesion, a clear shared goal. Everyone supported and helped each other, and it was a very informal process. We simply developed creative solutions as the need arose. We were good at noticing and celebrating when something went well (and it often did). We also did loads of mad and fun things together, both inside and outside the workplace, which created a great sense of community.

The actual premises we occupied weren't that much nicer than the ones in my previous job, but that wasn't really important because the psychosocial environment was so good. And at least I had a window.

I'm sure you've also experienced workplaces where you've been happy – and where you've been less than happy. Some just fill you with energy and make you look forward to being at work again when the weekend comes to an end. And others simply drain you. The type of working environment you're happy in can, of course, vary considerably between people. Even though I clearly prefer the second of the environments I've just described, perhaps it might be the opposite for someone else. For me it was a perfect environment. I absolutely loved it, felt alive there and grew professionally. But perhaps someone who was more dependent on structure, order and clear routines, and who preferred a serious workplace, would have felt it to be chaotic and lacking in focus.

Even though we might have different preferences when it comes to the working environment, most of us can agree on the characteristics common to good ones. Let's take a closer look at the various aspects of the working environment and what you and your colleagues can do together to create a really fantastic one for yourselves.

Physical, organisational and social working environment

The working environment is often divided into three parts: physical, organisational and social.

- *The physical working environment consists of everything from premises, furniture, machines and protective helmets to sound, light and ventilation.*

- *The organisational working environment involves how the work is organised and controlled, communication paths and how decisions are made.*

- *The social working environment is how we interact with and are affected by the people around us, such as our colleagues and boss.*

Another common expression is psychosocial working environment. This refers to how the individual themselves perceives and reacts to their surroundings. In other words, this relates to the individual's own subjective experiences – something that can be difficult for an employer to control. For this reason, the terms 'organisational working environment' and 'social working environment' have become more common.

We will be looking more closely at all of these aspects, but I've chosen to emphasise the social environment – in other words, how we interact with each other – because this is the aspect that we have the greatest possibility of affecting, regardless of the role we have at work.

Not just health or sickness

Today there's a great deal of focus on the working environment – above all on the organisational and social aspects. After all the alarming reports on the enormous increase in mental illness as a result of stress and other occupational health and safety problems, the majority of us probably agree that our working environment has a very significant influence on us.

Much of the legislation in the occupational health and safety field relates to the employer's responsibility for removing risks and preventing accidents and illness. And of course this is very important. But I think we should set even higher demands on our working environment. We don't automatically achieve an optimal working environment simply by removing any health risks. "How are you getting on in your new job?" "It's great, thanks, really a wonderful place to work. I haven't injured myself or burned out, and nobody's harassing me."

I think we can expect a little more than this. Imagine if we could appreciate how important the working environment is not only in terms of how we feel, but also in terms of how we *perform* and *develop*.

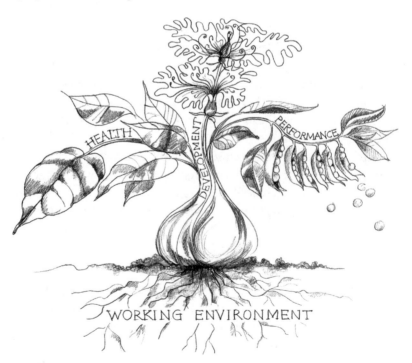

Just as in classic self-help literature, I believe that in working life, we often view performance and development as something that's only related to the individual – something that stems from our own motivation, willpower and driving force. But as I wrote in the introduction, if we only work with the individual and ignore the environment, we're only doing half of the job!

Your environment is crucial to whether you succeed in what you undertake, and that's just as true for the working environment. A beneficial working environment makes it easy for you and your colleagues to perform well and develop. A really good working environment makes it fun and easy to work. It means you can spend your energy on the right things and helps you as a team to achieve your shared goals and you as an individual to meet your personal objectives. And all without having to wear yourselves out. A beneficial environment gives you a helping hand so that you can be 'intelligently lazy'. So let's look at the working environment from a slightly broader perspective; one that includes all of these components – health, development and performance.

Leave that to the Health & Safety people

As I wrote earlier, many people seem to think it's up to the manager to ensure a a proper working environment. And of course your boss or manager does have considerable responsibility for it. But we all have a duty to contribute to a good working environment.

I also often hear comments like, "Oh, occupational health and safety issues are so boring. Can't we just leave all that to the safety representative?" But I think this is to only consider the 'negative', problem-oriented, aspect of occupational health and safety, where you try to identify and address risks, problems and shortcomings. And that's only part of the process. It's just as important to identify success factors and health-promoting factors. I think that if our working environment is the basis both for how we feel and how we perform and develop, and if it can make it either difficult or easy for us, then we should all consider this to be an extremely important area to be engaged in!

Imagine if you and your colleagues were to sit down and discuss how you could jointly create a really optimal working environment – not simply an acceptable one, where you don't fall sick, but a phenomenal working environment that helps you to truly flourish, be happy and feel great – an environment in which you bring out the best in each other and give each other mutual help to perform at the top of your game and reach your shared goals. I find it hard to believe that this kind of dialogue would be boring! A lot of the conversation would be about how you want to act towards each other, and how you want to collaborate, support, inspire and help each other to succeed.

Even if you aren't the manager, you can take the initiative and suggest such a dialogue. Of course, the ideal situation is where you bring your manager along with you in the dialogue, because the manager has more opportunities to affect aspects such as the physical and organisational environments. But you and your colleagues undoubtedly have ideas and suggestions that your manager hasn't even thought of. And when it comes to the social working environment, everyone can make just as much of a contribution. It's shaped by all of the people who work together, regardless of the role you occupy. So start talking about the working environment with your colleagues – it's much too important an issue to simply delegate it to your manager and the safety representative. You all need to be involved and agree how you can create a phenomenal environment in your workplace.

Chapter 8 contains concrete information you can use for this. There, I show you how you can use the same methodology to develop the working environment that you've already used to develop your own personal environments.

Take your working environment to a whole new level

What characterises a really good working environment? The basic requirement is of course that you should feel secure and safe and that you aren't injured or made sick by your working environment. Most countries' employment legislation contains rules about this, so I won't be looking at this in more detail here.

What I do want to focus on is how we take the working environment to even higher levels than the legislation requires, and how we make it truly optimal. How we make an environment that contributes not only to health and well-being, but also to development and good performance.

Creating a good physical working environment

If we start with the physical working environment, we can draw on a great deal of modern knowledge about how to optimise it. Of course, the basic requirement is that the physical environment should be secure and safe so that we don't risk injuring ourselves. It should also be functional and help us to be as effective as possible. It should be adapted to the type of activity that will take place on the premises, and it should give us the best possible conditions for feeling good and performing our best.

– Beauty and nature

In the book *Neurodesign*,[45] brain researcher Katarina Gospic and interior designer Isabelle Sjövall carry out a thorough review of how different aspects of the physical environment affect both our health and performance. They explain, for example, that if you experience your environment as beautiful and harmonious, a calm reaction is triggered in your body. You simply feel better in attractive environments – science has proven that they reduce your heart rate and lower your blood pressure. Of course, what we perceive

---

45 Gospic & Sjövall (2016)

to be beautiful varies between people. In general, we are drawn to symmetry and also prefer soft, rounded forms to hard, sharp ones.

Because being outdoors makes us feel so good, it's a good idea to try to get as much of nature into your working environment as possible. Natural views, pictures of the natural world on the walls and plants in the office increase job satisfaction and well-being, reduce tiredness and stress, make us healthier and more focused and increase productivity.

– Different environments are best for different tasks

Different types of environment are good for different types of task. Rooms with high ceilings are best for abstract, creative thinking. Low ceilings are best for concrete, specific thinking and good for detail-focused work. In other words, if you're an artist and you want full access to your creativity, you need a studio with a high ceiling. But if you're a surgeon, you can benefit from working in a room with a low ceiling. The same applies if you're an accountant and want to keep track of lots of figures.

Perhaps you can't affect the ceiling height in your workplace, but it can be useful to know that it isn't the actual ceiling height that's most important, but your experience of the room. And you can affect this with colours and decoration. For example, painting the entire room white makes it feel more spacious, as it blurs the boundaries between the floor, walls and ceiling, and the room feels bigger. You get the opposite effect if you paint the ceiling or floor in dark colours.

Colours also affect us in different ways. Red and green stimulate physical activity. Red can also give you a touch more stress, making you more alert. Blue is perceived as more calming. Green promotes creativity, perhaps because of our love of nature and because a positive mood increases creativity.[46]

---

46 The tips on ceiling height and colours are taken from Gospic & Sjövall (2016)

– Minimise disruptive noise and distractions

Light and sound also affect us. Bright environments, ideally
with real sunlight, improve performance. Today it's common
to have open-plan offices of various types. The disadvantage
of this is that we're exposed to more disruptive noise, and this
kind of noise from your surroundings can reduce productivity by
66% if you're working in an open-plan office. This is because it
becomes more difficult and requires more energy to concentrate
on your own task while your colleagues around you are talking
to each other or on the telephone. One study showed that we
are interrupted as we work on average every 11 minutes, and
that it takes about 25 minutes to regain your original focus. This
means that we can never work in a completely focused way.[47]

Of course this is a major problem, and a number of researchers
have noted that open-plan offices aren't intended for tasks that
require focus and thought.[48] According to Gospic & Sjövall,
different types of task are affected to different extents by
disruptive noise and other distractions. If you're working on
something that requires complete focus, your performance is
significantly impaired if you're exposed to lots of disruptions
that steal your energy. But if you're doing simpler tasks that
don't require as much thinking, it's not so serious if you're
surrounded by distractions. And how strongly you're affected
also depends on your own personality. Professor Daniel Stokols,
a researcher in the field of environmental psychology, says
that what he calls *high sensation seekers* – in other words,
people who want a lot of stimulation – are more tolerant and
less stressed by noisy, chaotic environments than *low sensation
seekers* – people who prefer a calmer and more secure existence.[49]

To reduce problems with noise and disruptions in open-plan
offices, Gospic & Sjövall suggest outfitting the workspace with
plenty of textiles, such as carpets and curtains and padded,
fabric-covered furniture. You can also install sound-absorbent tiles

47 Gospic & Sjövall (2016)
48 Kaarlela-Tuomaala (2009)
49 Stokols (2014)

on the ceiling. Consider which sounds you're adding to the environment and turn off or reduce the volume on things like telephones. Move printers, photocopiers, microwave ovens or coffee makers to a separate room, and agree on rules for conversations taking place in the shared space.[50]

One of the most important things we can do to improve our physical environment thus appears to be providing silence and separation, ensuring that we don't get interrupted the whole time. If you're working in an open-plan office and don't have any opportunity to affect this, you can at least make sure there are separate conversation rooms for telephone calls and physical meetings, and you can also discuss what can be done to minimise disruptive noise and interruptions.

– Environments that promote teamwork, interaction and recreation

How we decorate and furnish a room doesn't only affect our experience but also our social behaviour. According to Daniel Stokols, both outdoor and indoor environments can be designed so they bring people together and encourage social interaction, or so they keep people apart. For example, if you create small groups of furniture, this promotes social interaction, while if you place the furniture against the walls or so that people have their backs to each other, this reduces interaction. In other words, if you want to encourage teamwork and collaboration, it can be a good idea to furnish accordingly and to create lots of natural meeting places such as small, cosy groups of sofas or armchairs.

Stokols explains that before environmental psychology made a breakthrough in the 1950s and 1960s, investments in making the working environment more pleasant were seen as unnecessary costs. Research in the field of environmental psychology has helped companies and organisations understand the importance of the working environment. Today many organisations invest large sums in creating a really good physical environment for their

50 Gospic & Sjövall (2016)

employees. Companies such as Google, Pixar and Facebook have fantastically inviting and creatively decorated offices. This includes investments in designing environments for recreation and spontaneous meetings between employees, with things like ping-pong tables, basketball pitches, billiard tables and cosy seating areas. In its Zürich offices, Google has created a meditation room with couches, subdued lighting and large aquariums set into the walls.[51]

– Simple ways to increase satisfaction

Of course, these examples from Google, Facebook and Pixar are expensive, luxury offices that are probably far beyond the budget of the place where you work. But creating a cosy, inviting environment at work needn't cost a fortune. One easy way to improve satisfaction is to personalise the physical working environment a little more. We often set our own personal stamp on our homes, with paintings, photos and other meaningful items. And these things have an effect on us. Researchers have shown that students who decorate their student rooms with personal photos and other possessions more often complete their studies, while those who don't make any changes in their rooms and simply leave them cold and impersonal more often abandon their studies.[52]

In the workplace too, it's quite easy to personalise the physical environment so that it says something about the people working there and what they do. For example, you can hang up pictures of all the employees, display diplomas and awards, or show off images of the projects you've worked on. There's nothing that says a workplace has to be sterile and impersonal. Think about how you and your colleagues make your homes pleasant and welcoming. Which of these ideas can you use in the workplace?

When I worked in the grey concrete colossus I described earlier, I got together with another newly employed colleague and we did everything we could to transform the incredibly depressing physical environment into a more pleasant, inspiring one. Despite the fact that the 'old guard' sniggered and called it nonsense, we

51 Stokols (2014)
52 Stokols (2014)

stood up for ourselves and hung up textiles that we bought cheaply at IKEA. We brought in branches, twigs and stones from the forest outside, we arranged plants, colourful pictures and stimulating educational aids like koosh balls and bendeez.[53] And with these simple means, we succeeded in creating a really good physical environment that was appreciated both by ourselves and the course participants. In the end, even the old guard stopped complaining. Some of them even said that it had turned out really well.

REFLECTION: *What does the physical working environment look like in your workplace?*

- What's the physical environment like where you work?

- Do you have an environment that you experience as attractive and harmonious? Are you inspired and made more creative by your working environment?

- Is there a good noise level?

- Is the furniture and decoration functional? Does the environment facilitate the type of tasks you do, and your way of working?

- Is nature present in the environment in some way, for example in the form of potted plants, a view of the outdoors, paintings of the natural world or a green outdoor environment?

- What can you do yourself or together with your colleagues to make your physical working environment more pleasant?

Creating a good organisational and social working environment

Let's now look more closely at the organisational and social working environment. As I wrote earlier, the organisational environment is about how the work is organised and controlled,

---

53 A koosh ball is a ball made of rubber filaments that's nice to hold in your hand and fiddle with. Bendeez are a kind of bendy rubber rod that can be bent into a variety of shapes. Both give tactile stimulation that calms the mind and increases concentration. They were very popular in the education field in the late 1990s and early 2000s.

how the communication pathways work and how decisions are
made, and the social working environment involves how we
interact with and are affected by the people around us, such as our
colleagues and managers. These aspects are often closely linked
in practice, so I've chosen to discuss them in the same section.

When we look at the organisational and social working environment, a number of factors are usually emphasised. Here are some
of the most important ones:

FACTORS
relating to the ACTUAL WORK and WORKING SITUATION

- *Feeling pride in your own work, your team and your
  organisation*

- *Understanding the context – seeing where your own
  work fits into the overall picture*

- *Getting feedback, confirmation and feeling seen*

- *Influence and opportunities to have an impact, above all
  on your own working situation*

- *Opportunities for stimulation, variation, to learn things
  and develop*

- *Opportunities to use your strengths at work*

- *A balance between demands and resources – a feeling
  of control*

- *Clear goals and frameworks for your work*

- *A balance between work and leisure time*

FACTORS
relating to the SOCIAL CLIMATE in the workplace

- *Opportunities for conviviality and social contact*

- *Trust between colleagues and between employees
  and managers*

> *– Feeling respected and fairly treated*

> *– Being happy in the group, feeling a sense of fellowship and community*

> *– Feeling safe, getting support and help and daring to fail*

This is a simplified list that I could make even longer. But the most important components in a good working environment can actually be summarised in just two words: **Results** and **relationships**.[54] These two concepts cover pretty much everything in the above lists. Let's take a closer look at what they mean.

– *Results and relationships*

Results means feeling that you're making a contribution, that you're doing a good job, creating a good outcome and being able to take pride in your performance. And simultaneously being able to look around and take pride and joy in your colleagues' performances and your shared successes. You also need confirmation from other people, appreciation both from your manager and from your colleagues and customers – an acknowledgement that you're doing a good job.

"Happiness lies in the joy of achievement and the thrill of creative effort."

FRANKLIN D ROOSEVELT

---

54 See, for example, Kjerulf (2014) and Malmström & Skoglund (2013)

Relationships relates to wanting to be part of a social community and to feel fellowship with your colleagues. As humans, we have a basic need to belong to a group. We also really want to like the people we work with, and for them to like us. For our ancestors, belonging to a group was a matter of life or death – everyone knew that if you were excluded, you died. It's not quite that serious today, but we still feel the same fear. This is why harassment, exclusion and discrimination are among the worst things we can do to another person.

In other words, we want to do a good job and we want to be part of a social community. Take note of the fact that only one of these factors isn't enough to create a good working environment. Both of them must be present. A workplace that only focuses on results risks being an unpleasant place to work, and if people begin to dislike their workplace even the results will suffer. Meanwhile, a workplace that only focuses on relationships will undoubtedly be a pleasant place to work for a while, but not much will get done and in the end this can create frustration and boredom. However, if there is a focus on both results and relationships, these can combine to create a fantastic working environment.

The fact is that in studies, all of the other factors affecting the working environment have been shown to have less impact on how people perceive their workplace and how strong a sense of job satisfaction is created. Results and relationships can even outweigh a poor physical working environment. If your workplace is good in terms of these aspects, you'll probably feel that it's worth continuing to go to work and making an effort there day after day, even if the physical environment is really poor. Of course, this doesn't mean that you should ignore the physical working environment, but that the efforts you make in these areas will give the greatest effect.[55]

I can confirm this myself. Perhaps you remember the example I wrote about at the start of the chapter – the pleasant, slightly eccentric workplace I had after the grey concrete colossus.

55 Malmström & Skoglund (2013)

The physical working environment was really boring, but it didn't have much of an impact. We had such a great sense of community, we supported and helped each other so much to do a good job, and had such fun together, that it more than compensated for the dull offices we were working in.

In the same way that we did there, you and your colleagues can also do a great deal yourselves to help each other perform better and create good results, and so that you can experience the joy and security of being part of a social community. A lot of this is about the social working environment – in other words, how you act towards each other and the atmosphere and culture you create yourselves in your workplace. You probably already have lots of thoughts and ideas about this, but I'll end this chapter by giving you a few more suggestions for what you can do.

These ideas all have in common the fact that they contribute to creating a positive atmosphere. Today we have a lot of research showing that people need to be in a positive environment for them to truly be able to flourish, feel good, perform well and achieve good results. Barbara Fredrickson, one of the foremost researchers within the field of positive psychology, has demonstrated many effects of positive emotions. I mentioned this in the description of the Soul environment in Chapter 5. For example, when we're in a positive emotional state, we become more creative and better at solving complex problems. We see more opportunities and solutions, and find it easier to take in new knowledge and learn new skills. We're also better at collaborating with other people and creating new relationships, and we perform better.[56] In other words, it's a good idea to try to create the conditions for as many positive feelings as possible at work.

---

56 Fredrickson (2011)

Here are my suggestions for more positivity, better results and
healthier relationships.

- *Spread a positive infection*
- *See, include and care about each other*
- *Help each other to succeed*
- *Adopt an appreciative approach*
- *Explore and learn from your successes*
- *Make the most of your strengths*

Let's take a closer look at each of these suggestions.

– *Spread a positive infection*

It's often said that we're each other's working environment. And
that's quite true. How you and your colleagues act towards each
other and the culture, standards and values you create together are
a really important aspect of the working environment. Perhaps
even the most important.

Think about the colleagues you've most liked in your various
workplaces. What did they do that made them such a good part of
your working environment? Now think about yourself for a while.
What do you think it's like to have you as a working environment?
How do you affect your colleagues? Are you a resource that gives
them support, inspiration and impetus, helping them to succeed,
or are you the person that drains their energy and holds them
back? Or perhaps you're neither, but instead quite neutral?

I don't believe anyone wakes up in the morning and thinks,
"Right, today I'm going to be as obstructive as I possibly can to
the people I work with!" I imagine that most of us actually wish
each other well. But I think that sometimes we'd benefit from
looking at ourselves and asking these questions. Perhaps I don't
particularly like my job. Perhaps I've got stuck in a job that I

should have left long ago. If so, how does that affect my mood? And how does my mood affect the people around me?

Sometimes I have the participants in my talks do a little experiment to illustrate how much we affect each other. They divide into pairs, and have to look each other in the eyes for ten seconds. One person is instructed to try to stay completely neutral and not to change their facial expression, while the other is told to give their partner a big, genuine smile, and to continue smiling for ten seconds.

The results are always the same. The majority of the people who're supposed to be neutral almost immediately begin to smile or laugh. They simply can't control their own behaviour, but are infected by their partner's smile.

Why is that? Well, in the late 1990s a group of Italian researchers discovered something in the human brain that they called mirror neurons. These are specialised brain cells that recognise and then copy another person's emotions, actions and bodily sensations. These mirror neurons mean that our emotions are extremely infectious. And the copied emotions often lead to copied actions. When a stranger on a train yawns in front of you, you've probably found it impossible to resist doing the same. Or have you ever watched a TV programme in which someone runs into a door or has something thrown at their face, and found yourself shouting "Ouch" and holding your hands up to your own face? That's the mirror neurons in action.[57]

I once read about an experiment in which a group of people were observed as they waited for a train. One of them was part of the research team, but the others on the platform were unaware of this fact. That person began to act as if they were stressed. They bounced nervously up and down, tapped their foot and kept looking at their watch. After only a short time more than half of the other people on the platform began to behave in exactly the same way, bouncing, tapping their feet or looking at their watches.

So what do you think happens if you run around your

57 Achor (2011)

workplace and behave as if you're really stressed? And
what do you think happens if you go around sighing and
saying how awful everything is? You're pretty obviously
going to infect everyone else. Psychologist Daniel Goleman
compares this with passive smoking and says that we infect
innocent people around us with our negative emotions.[58]

Of course, I don't mean you should keep a false smile glued
to your face the whole day, but we need to be conscious of
how we affect each other and do what we can to contribute
to an atmosphere that makes us happy and feel good.
Everyone can have a bad day, and that's perfectly OK. But
is it OK to have a bad week? A bad month? Or a bad year?
And to constantly spread your bad mood to other people?

In any case, I prefer to be among people who do their best to
spread happiness around themselves and to infect other people
with positive emotions. It's been shown that if just one person
in a group is clearly happy and positive, it infects the entire
group. And that leads to fewer conflicts, better collaboration
and to the group performing better.[59] In the same way, studies
of sports teams have demonstrated that just one happy, positive
player is enough to infect the mood of the entire team, and
that the better the mood of the team, the better they play.[60]

Unfortunately, negative emotions are even more infectious
than positive ones, probably because humans have a genetic
attraction to negative things.[61] Those of our ancestors who simply
ran around on the savannah and thought positively didn't have
particularly long lives. They were quickly eaten by dangerous
animals or clubbed down by rival groups. It was our ancestors
who were more alert and more aware of threats, risks and
dangers who survived and transferred their genes onwards. And
those are the genes we carry today. Psychologists call this the
negativity bias, which means that our brains find it easier to both
notice and remember negative things than positive ones. This
means that stress, frustration, fear and anger in the workplace

58 Goleman (2006)   60 Totterdell (2000)
59 Barsade (2002)   61 Kjerulf (2014)

are more infectious than happiness, and so we need to make a conscious effort to spread happiness and positivity instead.

What's the atmosphere like in your workplace? What emotions and attitudes do you want to surround yourself with? Take responsibility for spreading those emotions – your emotions infect other people and spread outwards, and they also spread back to yourself. It becomes a positive spiral.

– See, include and care about each other

Be kind and thoughtful towards your colleagues. This perhaps sounds banal and self-evident, but imagine if we all followed this simple rule. We'd never need to make much more of an effort. Strive to make sure that everyone feels seen, included and appreciated. Ask how they feel, show interest, listen to and care about them.

Perform small, random acts of kindness – a well-known psychological exercise that contributes to positive emotions in both the giver and receiver. This could be something like getting a cup of coffee for a colleague, leaving a treat on someone's desk or sticking a Post-it note with an encouraging message on someone's computer screen.

"If you want to lift yourself up, lift up someone else."

BOOKER T. WASHINGTON

Small, simple things like saying a happy "Good morning", "Goodnight" and "Have a nice weekend" shouldn't be underestimated. A coaching client I had a few years ago told me that in his workplace nobody ever greeted anyone else in the morning. He thought it was a very sad place, so he decided to act as a good example and try to infect the other people. He began greeting his colleagues happily every morning. And he didn't settle for simply saying "Hello" or "Good morning", but also added something extra, like "Nice to see you", "How're things?", "How did it go yesterday", and perhaps even a pat on the shoulder or a high five. At the end of the day he said "Goodnight" to as many people as possible, and at the weekend he'd say "Have a nice weekend". He described how, for the first few days, his colleagues looked very surprised, but said that it didn't take more than a few days before some of them started to copy him. After a few weeks he'd got everyone doing the same and had created a completely different atmosphere in the workplace. And the thing he found the most fun was that it didn't stop with these small phrases of greeting. When his colleagues had really begun to open up, he soon heard more happy chatter and encouraging comments.

Taking a coffee break together and having time for a bit of small talk about things other than work also reinforces a sense of community. Get to know each other as people, not merely as colleagues, and do fun things together now and then to reinforce inclusion.

In the workplace I described earlier, the one characterised by 50% professionalism and 50% madness, we did lots of weird and fun things together, both inside and outside work.

One of the traditions we introduced was what we called our pay day vigil, and it went like this: on the evening of the 24th of every month, we got together at the home of one of our colleagues to await the arrival of our salaries. We ate something nice, socialised and had fun, and immediately before midnight we set off in a procession to the nearest cash point. There we lit outdoor candles, hung up balloons and streamers and other decorations. These could be Christmas decorations or anything that gave the occasion a festive feeling. And then we stood in a queue and each took out the first €10 of our newly arrived salary, to cheers and applause from the others.

We also had a Friday coffee break that we took it in turns to be responsible for, each with a different theme. One such Friday that I remember particularly well was when some of my colleagues arranged a coffee break with a 70s theme. When we were allowed into the room, we were met by disco music, a whirling mirror ball on the ceiling and the organisers dressed in flared trousers and afro wigs. They served Pommac, a typical Swedish drink from the 1970s, together with crisps and Twiglets, and the portly manager, who was about 60, strutted his stuff with a Travolta-inspired dance.

Feel free to adopt these ideas if you think that your colleagues would enjoy a pay day vigil or disco coffee break. Or get together to think up another fun activity. But remember that we are all different and that this type of activity may not suit everyone. So make sure you have some variation in the kind of things you do so that everyone feels welcome and included.

– Help each other to succeed

Many organisations have different forms of prizes and awards that they give to their best employees, often to the people who have performed best. Instead of doing this, the company Next Jump awards its most prestigious prize, The Avengers Award, to the person who has been the most helpful to their colleagues and cared most about the success of the group as a whole. Their aim is always to live up to the motto "Alone we can do good, together we can do great".[62]

This is something we can all copy. Imagine what a difference it would make to work in an organisation where the culture was

---

62 www.nextjump.com

characterised by helpfulness and collaboration, rather than strife and competition. And we can all contribute to such a culture. Be helpful and generous with both your time and your knowledge. Support each other so that everyone has the best possible conditions in which to do a good job. This way, you lift the entire team. And it also creates good results for the business. According to Cim Cameron, a professor in management and organisation, the most successful organisations create a culture that encourages good actions such as helping each other, being generous, sharing information and forgiving others when they make mistakes.[63]

In Sweden, the Westander PR agency has received a great deal of attention for its systematic investment in creating what it calls a culture of kindness within the company. A culture based on the fact that all of the employees actively and consciously help and support each other and collaborate to achieve the best for the group. This isn't a company where they want sharp-elbowed consultants, and there are no internal competitions. The culture of kindness permeates everything from how they recruit to how they have designed their salary and bonus system. Salaries and bonuses aren't merely affected by individual results, but also by how much the person helps their colleagues to achieve their goals. According to CEO Patrik Westander, being kind doesn't mean being cowardly, afraid of conflict or unwilling to make demands. Instead, it's about wishing other people well.[64]

Part of helping each other to succeed is also helping each other to dare to fail. If you work for an organisation where you all feel that it's OK to make a mistake and that you'll get help putting it right, this helps you both to find more creative solutions and to avoid wasting energy on concealing mistakes or finding excuses to avoid criticism. Encourage each other to try out different ways of doing things, dare to make mistakes and also to own up to them. We can all learn from our errors, and it builds confidence if every path is possible.

---

63 Lewis (2011)
64 www.westander.se

– *Explore and learn from your successes*

I think it's even more important to learn from your successes than it is to learn from your failures. Many workplaces put far too much emphasis on the things that don't work and on looking for errors, shortcomings, problems, deviations and failures. One workplace I visited had an enormous whiteboard on wheels standing in the middle of the open-plan office, clearly visible from everyone's desk. At the top of the whiteboard it said "Reported errors" and the whole thing was covered with errors, shortcomings, deviations and other misfortunes. "So where's the 'Things we got right' board?" I asked the manager who was showing me around. He gave me a sheepish look and mumbled, "Yeah, we actually don't have one of those..."

And unfortunately they aren't alone. Despite the fact that in most workplaces, people do far more things right than wrong, the focus isn't on the good results but on the things that didn't go so well. This risks creating a negative atmosphere, bringing people down and making us feel like we're failures. Often we don't just do this on an organisational level, we do it towards ourselves too. And then we really can't get the best out of ourselves or each other.

Instead, focus on the things that are going well. Pay attention to your good results. Be pleased for your colleagues, praise each other and celebrate your successes. And take the opportunity too to learn something about what causes success. Highlight positive examples and investigate why they worked so well. When someone succeeds particularly well with a task, explore together what it was that made it so successful, so that the whole group can benefit from that knowledge in future. When you want to be even better at something, you can think about the times when you've previously succeeded the most and explore what you did then. Share your experiences and learn from each other's successes. In this way, you create a positive atmosphere in which people can feel proud of their performance and results. You'll also generate lots of useful, creative ideas for how you can do even more of what you do well, and this is guaranteed to lead to both increased job satisfaction and still better results.[65]

– Adopt an appreciative approach

An appreciative approach means that you strive to see the good in the people surrounding you instead of looking for faults in them and that you show your appreciation and are generous with praise when your colleagues do good things.

"What you say to yourself
before you look at something
determines what you see."

ALBERT EINSTEIN

We're all heroes in our own stories. When I do something that turns out wrong, I know that I had good intentions and that I didn't mean anything bad. But when someone else makes a mistake or does something that affects us negatively, we have a tendency to believe that the person is malicious and has done it deliberately. Instead try to assume that just like you, other people usually have good intentions and mean well. Even if things sometimes turn out wrong, it's actually very rare for someone to wish you ill.

Don't waste so much energy on minor problems. Of course you should express criticism if someone makes a serious error or behaves really badly. But focus more on what does work than on what doesn't. Notice what your colleagues do right and well and reinforce what you want to see more of by paying attention to and praising it. Often it leads to better results if you reinforce the good things than if you complain about the negative stuff. If the

---

65 This approach is a foundation in strength-based development methods such as Appreciative Inquiry and Solution Focus.

basic atmosphere in the workplace is appreciative, encouraging and friendly, it's also easy to both give and receive criticism when it's deserved. Remember too that criticism can be formulated in different ways. A good way is to transform your complaints into wishes. Say what you want to see more of, rather than less of.

– *Make the most of your strengths*

Many of us probably think that we have greatest room for development where we're at our weakest. This assumption in turn rests on another one, which is that we can all become equally good at anything. But a number of researchers assert that instead we should take the opposite approach. Every individual has unique and often established talents, and we have the greatest room to grow where we have our strengths. It's only by building on and developing our strengths that we can become really accomplished within a given area – never by remedying our weaknesses. Marcus Buckingham and Donald Clifton from Gallup say that far from being development, fixing our weaknesses is more about damage control. Of course we do have to spend time on this sometimes, especially if our weaknesses are getting in the way of good performance. But don't spend more time than necessary on your weaknesses. It's enough if you just bring them up to an acceptable level.[66]

It's our strengths that are our very biggest assets, for ourselves, those around us and for our employers. And that's why you and your colleagues should do everything you can to use and develop your strengths as much as possible. As I wrote in Chapter 5, in the section on the Personality environment, a strength isn't merely something you're good at. It's something you have a natural aptitude for, something that feels easy and fun to use. When you use a strength, it gives you energy and you feel like your 'true self'. You feel engaged and easily enter the flow state. You perform at the top of your game and can get lots of things done without it feeling like a particular effort. When someone utilises

66 Buckingham & Clifton (2005)

their strengths, it doesn't merely have positive effects for that individual. It's also been shown to lead to advantages for their organisation in the form of higher productivity, more satisfied customers, lower staff turnover and lower sickness absence.[67]

In Chapter 5 I also gave you a few tips on how to find your own strengths (see Environment no. 10: Personality). When you've found out what your strengths are, you need to use them as much as possible and find ways of developing them still further. You should also think about the strengths you have in your working group and how you can best utilise each individual's unique strengths. Perhaps you can find a way of dividing the work so that everyone gets to use their own strengths as much as possible.

The British company Cougar Automation encourages its employees to talk about the strengths they have in their team, and to divide the tasks between them so that each of them gets to do more of what most utilises their strengths. You don't need to make major changes; simply getting rid of something that drains you and adding something that you love makes an enormous difference. Cougar Automation has won a number of prizes for its excellent service, and their CEO Clive Hutchinson says that the most important secret behind their success is exactly this approach of systematically striving to utilise their employees' strengths – something that has led both to happier employees and more satisfied customers.[68]

"You need to be aware of what others are doing, applaud their efforts, acknowledge their successes, and encourage them in their pursuits. When we all help one another, everybody wins."

JIM STOVALL

---

67 Linley (2008), Buckingham & Clifton (2005)
68 Lewis (2011)

REFLECTION: *What does the organisational and social working environment look like in your workplace?*

- What's the atmosphere like in your workplace? Do you infect each other with positive or negative feelings?

- Do you care about each other and get everyone to feel seen and included in the social community?

- Do you help each other to succeed and create good results?

- Do you have an appreciative approach and focus on what your colleagues are doing right rather than on what they do wrong? Are you generous with praise?

- Do you talk about successes and good examples and learn from each other's positive experiences?

- Do you know the different strengths of the members of your team? Do you utilise them in the best possible way?

Summary

The working environment contains aspects of all of your personal environments. Part of your physical environment can be found at work, together with part of your relationship environment, your network and technology environments and so on. What makes the working environment special is that it's an environment you share with other people, and you and your colleagues therefore need to take account of and combine your needs and wishes about how you want your shared working environment to be. You're also all part of each other's working environment, which means that you need to think about how you can be as good an environment as possible for your colleagues.

In this chapter, we've seen that just like each of your personal environments, your working environment can make you flourish and feel full of life, or make you wither away and feel drained. I feel strongly that all of us, regardless of our role, should take greater responsibility for creating a really good working environment, and that we should raise the bar so that we aren't merely focusing on health and safety. An optimal working environment isn't merely one in which we don't fall sick. It's an environment that provides optimal conditions for people to flourish, be happy, develop and perform to their highest potential.

We've looked at how the physical working environment can be designed to promote satisfaction, well-being and good performance, and we've reviewed the most important components in a good organisational and social working environment: results and relationships. And finally, I've shared with you a number of tips on how you and your colleagues can create a really supportive social environment:

- *Spread a positive infection*

- *See, include and care about each other*

- *Help each other to succeed*

- *Adopt an appreciative approach*

- *Pay attention to and learn from your successes*

- *Make the most of your strengths*

What does this mean for you and your colleagues?

As you can see, there's a lot that you and your colleagues can do yourselves to create a really good working environment. You can use simple techniques to make your physical environment more pleasant and personal, and you can do lots of things to create a more positive, helpful and friendly atmosphere. You can help each other to perform and create good results, you can give each other appreciation and you can include everyone in your social community. You can highlight good examples, learn from your successes and utilise each other's strengths.

And this isn't even particularly difficult – quite the opposite. A lot of the things I've mentioned involve simply talking and agreeing about how you want to relate to and behave with each other. My experience from the workplaces I've seen that have used these strategies is that they're fantastic to be in. View these suggestions as inspiration for the dialogue that you and your colleagues will hopefully now have about your own working environment and how you can create a workplace that you look forward to when the weekend is drawing to a close.

In the next chapter I'll show you how you can use the same seven-step method as in Part Two, with concrete questions that you can discuss.

CHAPTER 7 | YOUR WORKING ENVIRONMENT

"Help create a work environment where it's easy for others to be happy at work."

ALEXANDER KJERULF

SEVEN STEPS FOR DESIGNING AN OPTIMAL WORKING ENVIRONMENT

In this chapter, I suggest an approach and some questions that you and your colleagues can use to decide together how you want your own dream environment to look and what you can do to create it. In Chapter 6 I went through a seven-step process that will help you review and change your personal environments. And with a few adjustments, you can use the same steps with your colleagues when you're discussing how to design an optimal working environment.

Below I give you a brief description of how to use these seven steps in your workplace. I've chosen to keep this part quite short, because you're already familiar with the method from having gone through it for your own personal environments. But if you've jumped directly to the working environment section, I recommend that before you read any further you go back and read Chapter 6, where I explain all seven steps in more detail. What's a little bit different about this chapter is that between steps 6 and 7 I've added a couple of headings about creating concrete action plans and following up the process.

I don't go into the various legal rules about carrying out inventories of risks and shortcomings or removing health hazards from the workplace. Of course these are important aspects of improving your working environment, and such things must be done – indeed they form part of Step 2, trashing your tolerations. But my primary focus here isn't carrying out a complete risk assessment. Instead I want to focus on how you can raise the bar still further and create not merely an acceptable working environment where you don't fall sick, but a truly phenomenal working environment that makes it easy and fun to be at work and achieve good results together with your colleagues.

At the end of the chapter you'll find all the steps in a section that you can copy and share with your colleagues (and your manager, who I hope will also take part) when you meet to talk about your working environment. Use this as a resource when you review your working environment as it is today, discuss how you want it to be and plan the changes you want to make to design a really beneficial environment. This section also has space for you to note down what you decide. When you've done this, you'll have a complete action plan.

As you go through the questions and tasks, I recommend that you talk about all parts of the working environment – physical, organisational and social. But it can be sensible to focus most on the social working environment, because this is the one that you all have the biggest opportunity to affect.

Foundations:
Goals, visions and guiding principles

In Chapter 4, you reflected on your own objectives, dreams and visions. You also formulated guiding principles. And you then used these as the starting point for your reflections about your own personal environment. I recommend that you do the same thing with your colleagues before you start with the seven steps.

What goals and visions are you at work to achieve? What are the organisation's goals? What are your work group's goals? What are your own goals?

Here, the guiding principles can equate to your organisation's values. Do you already have shared values? Do these primarily relate to how you act externally, towards customers and other interested parties, or do they also include how you act internally, how you treat each other, communicate and work together?

If you don't already have values, or if the ones you have only relate to how you treat your customers, it can be a good idea to develop values relating to how you approach each other inside your organisation. Suggest to your manager that you work together in the group to establish shared values. You can do the exercise (except for Step 1) even if you don't have any agreed core values that are written down. But I think you'll get more out of it if you have shared core values to work from.

Step 1: Let your guiding principles / values be reflected in your environment

The first step involves reviewing how your working environment corresponds to your guiding principles – in other words, your values. So for example if one of your values is 'generosity', do you think generosity permeates your working environment, your culture and how you act towards each other? Or are you instead unwilling to share and help each other?

If you don't see your values in your working environment, think about what you do see instead. What words would best summarise the current situation in your working environment?

Finally, discuss how you can make your working environment reflect your guiding principles. To continue with the above example, how can you make your working environment be characterised by 'generosity'? What does it mean to be generous and how can this be shown in your everyday work?

Think about how a really ideal working environment, one that truly reflects your guiding principles/values, would look. If you were going to design such an ideal environment, what would it mean to you? What would it mean in terms of your job satisfaction, well-being and your ability to achieve really good results?

Step 2: Trash your tolerations

The second step involves identifying and eliminating – or accepting – tolerations and obstacles in the working environment. Think about what irritates you, what you complain about and what drains your energy. This can be everything from annoying noises, complicated procedures and negative treatment to machines or tools that don't work properly, disorder and things that are broken.

– How do these tolerations affect your ability to achieve your goals?

Then discuss how you can get rid of them. What can you affect yourselves? What can you escalate to the right decision makers? What can you not affect at all? How do you deal with that? There may be some tolerations that you can't eliminate completely, but you need to find a way of accepting the ones you can't affect, so that you don't permit them to drain your energy.

Some tolerations can involve behaviours and treatment that you don't like. Dare to discuss this! But avoid personal attacks. Simply agree which behaviours aren't acceptable, and what you want to see instead.

Another important thing to reflect on is your different personalities. Sometimes tensions, irritations and conflicts arise simply because we are all different and we don't understand each other. But you can't get rid of your colleagues even if they annoy you. Instead, you need to think about how you can accept and even appreciate your differences.

Step 3: Cultivate your resources

The third step is about identifying the resources you have in your working environment. What's already good? What gives you energy and inspiration, support and impetus? Resources can be everything from efficient procedures, tools and systems to supportive behaviour, positive treatment, collaboration and what you focus on and draw attention to. They can also be things in the physical environment that contribute to making it easy to be happy at work and to creating great results. Try to find everything that contributes to both well-being and good levels of performance.

One way to identify your resources can be thinking about when you've experienced real high points at work – occasions when

you've felt really good, experienced balance, felt satisfied
and happy, committed and proud of yourself, your colleagues
and the work you do. Allow everyone in the group to talk about
a high point and discuss together what contributed to those
occasions feeling so good. Everything that contributed can be
seen as resources that you already have.

Then discuss how you can get even more benefit from your
resources, build on them and make them grow. Which of these
resources would you like to see even more of in your team or
organisation? What could make these resources even better?

Step 4: Add what's missing

The fourth step is about considering what's missing from
your working environment today. What additional resources
could you add that can give you even more support, energy,
inspiration and impetus?

This could be everything from helpful, supportive behaviour,
shared procedures that give you all a positive boost, or things in
the physical environment. You'd perhaps like to bring in more
potted plants, paintings or sound-absorbent textiles for the office,
introduce a positive check-in at the weekly meeting where you
all get to talk about something you've succeeded with in the last
week, or agree on new ways of helping and supporting each other.
Or something completely different.

Prioritise your ideas. What can you do yourselves, and what
ideas require a decision from higher up in the organisation before
they can move forwards? Appoint someone to communicate these
suggestions to the right decision makers.

Step 5: Experiment with your existing environments

The fifth step involves experimenting with your existing
environments. Try removing or adding something and see how

this feels and how it affects you. Approach the task with a child's
curiosity and playfulness. What would be fun to try out?

This could be everything from adding or doing away with a
meeting or reallocating some of your tasks to having a shared
break time every morning for a week or hanging up pictures
in the conference room.

The whole idea of experimenting is that you don't have to
stick with the change – simply try it out and see what happens.
If it doesn't work, you can always change it back.

Step 6: Try out entirely new environments

The previous step, experimenting with your existing environments,
means that you try out something new in an environment you're
already familiar with and feel at home in. The sixth step, trying
out entirely new environments, is a bigger one, where you go
outside your habitual, safe and comfortable environments and
try out an environment you haven't previously experienced.

This could involve something like introducing walking
meetings, where you go outdoors and talk as you move. I think
this is one of the best ways to get your creativity going. It could
be a big change like moving the entire organisation or team to
different premises, or a smaller one such as allowing everybody
to work from wherever they want once a week – at work, from
home, from a café or somewhere else. And it needn't simply
involve changing environment in purely physical terms. It
can also mean starting a completely new partnership, whether
internally or externally, or acquiring new technical tools.

Try it out and see how it feels! And just like in the previous
step, you needn't stick with the new environments. Although
of course it can be difficult to change your mind if you move
the entire business to new premises.

Create action plans

Compile all of the suggestions and ideas you come up with in
steps 1-6. If necessary, choose those you think it's most important
to work on immediately. These will be your short-term goals for
the working environment.

Then draw up concrete action plans for the suggestions you'll
be working on:

- WHAT is to be done?

- WHEN should it be done?

- WHO is responsible?

Some of the suggestions are perhaps the kind of thing that you
can't really draw up an action plan for. For example, this could
be how you've agreed to treat each other. When it comes to
agreements like this, it's important instead to try to concretise
them as much as possible.

- For example, what does it mean to show respect (or
  whatever you've decided to do)? How do you do that
  in practice?

- How do you make sure you're sticking to the things you've
  agreed about, that these behaviours really become part of
  your culture and not merely pretty words on paper?

- How can you encourage and confirm positive behaviours
  and how do you signal when you think somebody isn't
  sticking to what you've agreed to do?

DOCUMENT what you've agreed.

Decide on A FIRST STEP you can take during the next week.

Following up and carrying on

Finally, agree how you're going to check back, follow up and keep the process alive. Creating a fantastic working environment isn't something you only do during one meeting and then it's done. It's a constant, ongoing process.

But if you've gone through the steps above, you've hopefully got off to a really good start. Having goals and action plans for the organisational and social working environment is also required for some ISO certifications.

Congratulations – you're already a good way towards designing your own optimal working environment! Remember to pay attention to and celebrate your progress. Maintain a positive focus – improving your working environment can and should be enjoyable.

Step 7: Adapt to your environments

When all the changes you've agreed on have become reality, and you've created a really beneficial working environment that gives you maximum support, inspiration and energy and helps you all in the right direction... well, there's only one thing left to do – adapt to the upgraded environment and allow it to help you move forwards.

In this step, you needn't do anything specific yourselves except act on the basis of the agreements you've come to. Now you can harvest the fruit of the work you did in the earlier steps.

If you've really succeeded in designing a good working environment, you'll soon notice how your energy and inspiration increase, how enjoyable it is to be at work, how you feel good, grow and develop and how you create fantastic results together. And without having to bend over backwards. The environment – which largely consists of all of the employees in your workplace – will give you a helping hand, just as if you were all sitting at the top of the slide I wrote about in the introduction, with your goals at the bottom of it.

– All you need to do is enjoy the ride.

On the following pages you'll find the steps and questions we've gone through above, with space to add your own notes.
Feel free to copy and share these pages.

Discussion prompts to copy
Our goals, visions and values

....

....

....

....

Step 1: LET YOUR GUIDING PRINCIPLES/VALUES BE REFLECTED IN THE ENVIRONMENT

HOW does your working environment correspond to your guiding principles – in other words, your values?

....

....

....

....

If you don't see your values in your working environment, what do you see instead? What WORDS would best summarise the CURRENT SITUATION in your working environment?

....

....

....

....

What can you DO to make your working environment reflect
your guiding principles?

....

....

....

....

What would an ideal working environment look like?
If you were going to DESIGN such an IDEAL environment,
what would it MEAN to you?
What would it mean in terms of your job satisfaction,
well-being and your ability to achieve really good results?

....

....

....

....

....

....

....

....

Step 2: TRASH YOUR TOLERATIONS

What OBSTACLES/TOLERATIONS are there in
your working environment?
Things that annoy you, that you complain about,
things that drain your energy.

....

....

....

....

....

....

....

How do these obstacles/tolerations AFFECT your ability
to achieve your goals?

....

....

....

....

....

....

How can you DO AWAY WITH them?
Which ones can you ELIMINATE completely and which ones
do you have no way of affecting?
How can you find a way to ACCEPT the latter, so that you don't
permit them to drain your energy?

....

....

....

....

....

....

Step 3: CULTIVATE YOUR RESOURCES

What resources do you have in your working environment?
What's ALREADY GOOD?

....

....

....

....

....

....

200   How can you GET EVEN MORE BENEFIT from your resources, build on them and make them grow?

....

....

....

....

....

....

....

Step 4: ADD WHAT'S MISSING

What's currently MISSING from your working environment? What additional resources could you add that can give you even more support, energy, inspiration and impetus?

....

....

....

....

....

....

....

Step 5: EXPERIMENT WITH YOUR EXISTING ENVIRONMENTS

What can you EXPERIMENT with in your existing environments?

....

....

....

....

....

....

Step 6: TRY OUT ENTIRELY NEW ENVIRONMENTS

Is there any NEW ENVIRONMENT you'd like to try out?
If so, which?

....

....

....

....

....

....

....

Action plan

WHAT is to be done?

....

....

....

....

....

WHO is responsible?

....

....

....

....

....

WHEN should it be done?

....

....

....

....

....

....

....

....

Decide on A FIRST STEP that you can take during the next week!

....

....

....

....

We'll FOLLOW UP how it goes and decide on the next step on the
FOLLOWING DATE:

....

....

....

Step 7: ADAPT TO YOUR ENVIRONMENTS

Congratulations! When you've created a really beneficial working
environment, there's only one thing left to do: Adapt to the
upgraded environment and allow it to help you move forwards!

CONCLUSION

Do you remember the tiny seed I wrote about in the introduction? A seed that has all the potential it needs to grow into a tall, flourishing tree – if it's planted in the right environment.

Imagine this large, magnificent tree before you. This tree has had every opportunity to grow and develop, with a strong trunk, stable roots that keep it firmly upright, innumerable branches reaching towards the sky and thousands of healthy green leaves.

Become that tree!

Make sure you plant yourself in as beneficial an environment as possible – an environment that helps you get the life you want and be the person you want to be. An environment where you're happy, where you feel good and which makes you develop in the direction you want. Get rid of all the weeds that threaten to stifle you, all the pests that cause you problems, and instead surround yourself with everything that feeds you, supports you and helps you to grow.

Do the same thing for your colleagues at work, and for your family and friends. Be a resource for them. Support and help them so that they too can grow into large, flourishing trees.

Why be satisfied with living a life like a dehydrated little bush when we all have the potential to be so much more? Why fight an uphill battle or struggle against a headwind when you can design environments, both at home and at work, that make you feel full of life, help you in the right direction and make the whole thing feel easy and fun?

Regardless of what a wonderful life, at home and at work, means for you – take the lazy (and intelligent) route to get there.

I wish you all the success in the world!

TO THE READER

Thank you for taking the time to read my book! I hope it's given you new and useful ideas, insights and tools.

If you'd like to contact me and tell me what you thought about the book, how it's affected you and the changes it's led to, you're very welcome to drop me a line at gunnel@rynerconsulting.se. I'd really love to hear from you.

– Would you like to know more about me and my work?

Please visit my website, gunnelryner.com, where you can read about my keynote speeches, training courses and workshops.

Best wishes,
Gunnel Ryner

www.gunnelryner.com
gunnel@rynerconsulting.se

*"The path to success
doesn't involve more willpower*

*— instead it involves creating
a truly favourable environment
and then allowing it to
do the hard work for you."*

GUNNEL RYNER

REFERENCES

BOOKS AND ARTICLES

Achor, Shawn (2011) *The Happiness Advantage. The Seven Principles that Fuel Success and Performance at Work.* Virgin Books.

Adam, Hajo & Galinsky, Adam D. (2012) *Enclothed cognition.* Journal of Experimental Social Psychology, 48(4):918-925.

Alexander, Bruce K. (2010) Addiction – *The View from Rat Park.* http://www.brucekalexander.com/articles-speeches/rat-park /148-addiction-the-view-from-rat-park (2017-01-05)

Alexander, Christopher (1979) *The Timeless Way of Building.* Oxford University Press.

Ariely, Dan (2010) *Predictably Irrational, Revised and Expanded Edition: The Hidden Forces That Shape Our Decisions.* HarperTorch.

Barsade, Sigal G. (2002) *The ripple effect: Emotional contagion and its influence on group behavior.* Administrative Science Quarterly, 47(4):644-675.

Baumeister, R. F., Bratslavsky, E., Muraven, M. & Tice, D. M. (1998) *Ego depletion: Is the active self a limited resource?* Journal of Personality and Social Psychology, 74(5):1252-1265.

Buckingham, Marcus & Clifton, Donald O. (2005) *Now, Discover Your Strengths. How to Develop Your Talents and Those of the People You Manage.* Pocket Books.

Christakis, Nicholas & Fowler, James (2010) *Connected. The Amazing Power of Social Networks and How They Shape Our Lives.* Harper Press.

Clayton, Susan D. & Saunders, Carol D. (2012) *The Oxford Handbook of Environmental and Conservation Psychology.* Oxford University Press.

Dawkins, Richard (1976) *The Selfish Gene.* Oxford University Press.

Dutton, Donald G. & Aron, Arthur P. (1974) *Some evidence for heightened sexual attraction under conditions of high anxiety.* Journal of Personality and Social Psychology. 30(4):510–517.

Flora, Carlin (2013) *Friendfluence: The Surprising Ways Friends Make Us Who We Are.* Doubleday.

Fredrickson, Barbara (2011) *Positivity. Groundbreaking Research to Release Your Inner Optimist and Thrive.* Oneworld.

Friedman, Howard S. & Martin, Leslie R. (2012) *The Longevity Project: Surprising Discoveries for Health and Long Life from the Landmark Eight-Decade Study.* Plume Books.

Frizell, Elsa (2017) *Ge en knuff i rätt riktning.* Personal & Ledarskap #1 2017, p. 10-13.

Goleman, Daniel (2006) *Social Intelligence: The New Science of Human Relationships.* Bantam.

Gospic, Katarina & Sjövall, Isabelle (2016) *Neurodesign: inredning för hälsa, prestation och välmående.* Bokförlaget Langenskiöld.

Guéguen N, Jacob C, Le Guellec H, Morineau T & Lourel M. (2008) *Sound Level of Environmental Music and Drinking Behavior: A Field Experiment With Beer Drinkers.* Alcoholism: Clinical and Experimental Research, 32(10):1795–1798.

Harford, Tim (2008) *The Logic of Life: The Rational Economics of an Irrational World.* Random House.

Hari, Johann (2015) *Chasing the Scream: The First and Last Days of the War on Drugs.* Bloomsbury USA.

IJzerman, Hans & Semin Gün R. (2009) *The Thermometer of Social Relations: Mapping Social Proximity on Temperature.* Psychological Science, 20(10):1214 – 1220.

Jonkman, Linus (2016) *Introvert: The friendly takeover.* National Library of Sweden.

Kaarlela-Tuomaala, A., Helenius, R., Keskinen, E., Hongisto, V. (2009) *Effects of acoustic environment on work in private office rooms and open-plan offices – longitudinal study during relocation.* Ergonomics, 52(11):1423-1444.

Kahneman, Daniel (2013) *Thinking, Fast and Slow.* Farrar, Straus and Giroux.

Kalb, Claudia (2008) *Drop That Corn Dog, Doctor.* Newsweek 13 Oct 2008.

Keller, Matthew et al (2005). *A warm heart and a clear head: The contingent effects of weather on human mood and cognition.* Psychological Science, 16:724-731.

Kjerulf, Alexander (2014) *Happy hour is 9 to 5. How to love your job, love your life, and kick butt at work.* PineTribe Ltd.

Leonard, Thomas (1998) *The Portable Coach: 28 Surefire Strategies for Business and Personal Success.* Scribner.

Lewis, Sarah (2011) *Positive Psychology at Work: How Positive Leadership and Appreciative Inquiry Create Inspiring Organizations.* Wiley-Blackwell.

Linley, Alex (2008) *Average to A+: Realising Strengths in Yourself and Others.* CAPP Press.

Little, William et al (2013) *Introduction to Sociology.* OpenStax College.

Livni, Ephrat (2016) *Trees Please. The Japanese practice of 'forest bathing' is scientifically proven to improve your health.* Quartz 2016-10-12, https://qz.com/804022/health-benefits-japanese-forest-bathing/.

Malmström, Clas & Skoglund, Lennart (2013) *Chefen som gör skillnad.* Gothia Förlag.

Michelson, William (1970) *Man and His Urban Environment: A Sociological Approach.* Addison-Wesley Educational Publishers Inc.

Myers, David G. (2014) *Exploring Social Psychology, 7th edition.* McGraw-Hill.

Neal, David T., Wood, Wendy & Quinn, Jeffrey M. (2006) *Habits—A Repeat Performance.* Current Directions in Psychological Science,15(4):198-202.

Nordfält, Jens (2007) *Marknadsföring i butik – Om forskning och branschkunskap i detaljhandeln.* Liber.

Parker-Pope, Tara (2007) *Will your resolutions last until February?* New York Times, 2007-12-31.

Petersson, Caroline (2014) *Nudging ska få oss att välja rätt.* Camino magasin, http://www.caminomagasin.se/nyheter/2014/02/12/nudging-ska-fa-oss-att-valja-ratt, 2014-02-12.

Seligman, Martin (2012) *Flourish. A Visionary New Understanding of Happiness and Well-being.* Free Press.

Søhoel, Synne & Hanssen, Kjetil (2016) *Manglerudhjemmet med pub, spa og restaurant: Plutselig har de ikke vondt i hoften lenger.* Aftenposten 29/08/2016.

Totterdell, Peter (2000) *Catching moods and hitting runs: Mood linkage and subjective performance in professional sports teams.* Journal of Applied Psychology, 85(6):848-859.

Ulrich, Roger S. (1984) *View through a window may influence recovery from surgery.* Science, 224(4647):420-421.

Wiseman, Richard (2010) *59 Seconds: Change Your Life in Under a Minute.* Anchor Books.

Next Jump's website, www.nextjump.com

Stokols, Daniel (2014) *Environmental Psychology*. Series of talks at the University of California, Irvine, UCI Media, https://www.youtube.com/ playlist?list=PLA2E69FC89640C272.

Svenskarna och internet 2016, www.soi2016.se

Westander's website, www.westander.se

REFERENCES

CPSIA information can be obtained
at www.ICGtesting.com
Printed in the USA
BVHW041206140419
545471BV00017B/489/P